The **Politically Incorrect Guide**™ to

The **Politically Incorrect Guide**™ to

The Sixties

❀ ❀ ❀ ❀ ❀

Since 1947
REGNERY
PUBLISHING, INC.
An Eagle Publishing Company • Washington, DC

Library of Congress Cataloging-in-Publication Data on file with the Library of Congress.

ISBN 978-1-59698-572-8

Published in the United States by
Regnery Publishing, Inc.
One Massachusetts Avenue, NW
Washington, DC 20001
www.regnery.com

Manufactured in the United States of America

10 9 8 7 6 5 4 3 2 1

Books are available in quantity for promotional or premium use. Write to Director of Special Sales, Regnery Publishing, Inc., One Massachusetts Avenue NW, Washington, DC 20001, for information on discounts and terms or call (202) 216-0600.

Distributed to the trade by:
Perseus Distribution
387 Park Avenue South
New York, NY 10016

To my parents, whose generosity, concern, and love
I only now begin to appreciate.

CONTENTS

Contents

INTRODUCTION

Was the 1960s a decade characterized by free love, drug binges, rock festivals, and radical politics? This, no doubt, is what Hollywood bigwigs and other elite groups want us to believe. In countless TV shows, movies, and even textbooks, the 1960s is depicted as a glorious time of widespread social rebellion, when young people rose up and overthrew the stale, square conventions of the past.

Take just one well-known event: the Beatles' 1964 appearance on the *Ed Sullivan Show*. This has been depicted with astonishing regularity as a pivotal cultural moment; in fact an entire movie—*I Wanna Hold Your Hand*—was built around it. And that Sullivan episode was indeed a major event in popular culture. But did you know that in 1961, 26 million people watched a CBS live broadcast of the first performance of a new symphony by classical composer Aaron Copland?[1] Moreover, with all the attention that sixties rock groups receive, it might come as a surprise to learn that *My Fair Lady* was Columbia Records' biggest-selling album before the 1970s, beating out those of sixties icons Bob Dylan, Janis Joplin, and the Byrds.[2]

In researching this book, I quickly discovered a surprising thing about the 1960s: the decade was not nearly as radical as we've been led to believe. In fact, the upheaval was really confined to a very narrow stratum of society. For the overwhelming majority of Americans, the 1960s was a conservative decade.

For example, I interviewed men who had been Communist agitators at schools like Harvard and Columbia in the late 1960s. They told me that women they dated—coeds who shared their extreme political views— would regularly tell them after a month or two of going steady that they wouldn't be sleeping together because the women were saving them- selves for marriage. I also learned that not only did these students wear ties and dress slacks to dinner every night, but that the clothes they wore at their protests typically came from Brooks Brothers.

And those were the radicals!

The most common adage about the decade is that if you remember any of the 1960s, you weren't there. Let's consider the source: pop musician Paul Kantner. During the 1960s, Kantner was a member of Jefferson Air- plane. Although the group is hailed as a quintessential sixties rock band, its repertoire of drug-addled psychedelia and anti-authority lyrics did not produce a single number one hit during the decade. (Two decades later, however, rechristened as Starship, the group would have three runaway number-one hits by serving up the blandest, most inane and unimagina- tive rock anthems possible, including musical travesties like "We Built This City.") In contrast, crooner Bobby Vinton had four number one hits in the 1960s, while becoming one of the most popular recording acts of the decade. Today, everyone thinks of Jefferson Airplane as a classic product of the 1960s, while Vinton is hardly remembered at all.

But was Kantner's experience really more authentic than Vinton's?

When we look at the American population overall, and not just the small group of radicals who dominate the history books, we find that the 1960s was one of the most conservative periods in American history. For most Americans, they were also a time of remarkable family cohesion. Divorce rates were low, illegitimacy rates were low, and premarital sex was more the exception than the rule.

The popular Hollywood stars of the 1960s were not rebellious outcasts or disaffected hippies, but straight-laced, all-American personalities. John Wayne and Julie Andrews were the biggest stars, followed by the likes of Doris Day, Rock Hudson, Sandra Dee, Paul Newman, Glenn Ford, Sean Connery, Cary Grant, Dean Martin, Tony Curtis, Sidney Poitier, and Jerry Lewis. Among the most-beloved teen idols were Fabian and the former Mouseketeer, Annette Funicello.

Even the decade's biggest sex symbols were comparatively modest and restrained. Refusing to do nude scenes, Elizabeth Taylor was positively chaste compared to today's willfully provocative starlets like the heavily tattooed Angelina Jolie. And the biggest male heartthrob of the 1960s was probably Elvis Presley, an unabashedly patriotic former GI who addressed interviewers and even his fans as "sir" and "ma'am." Starting in 1960, Elvis won three Grammy awards, all for gospel music—a lifelong passion of Elvis's that is not much discussed anymore. The titles of these LPs should tell you a good deal about the singer—and the period: "His Hand in Mine," "How Great Thou Art," and "He Touched Me."

Does all this suggest a period of widespread radical ferment and sexual license?

The 1960s was also a time when America's suburbs were growing rapidly. The ambition of most young people wasn't to do drugs, sleep around, and fight authority; it was to get married, move to a nice house in a quiet town, and start a family—and that's what most were doing.

This was not only true of middle-class whites, but of middle-class blacks as well. Although urban riots are one of the dominant images of race relations in the "turbulent" 1960s, for every black looter and arsonist there were many more black couples leaving urban areas for a better life and better schools in the suburbs. In the process, these families were peacefully integrating—without busing orders or demonstrations.

The small number of sixties leftwing radicals referred to themselves as the "counterculture" for a reason—they were reacting against a very conservative and very dominant mainstream culture. This conservatism also extended to popular attitudes toward the Cold War—as this book explains, polling revealed that most of those who voted for antiwar stalwart Eugene McCarthy in the 1968 Democratic primaries actually wanted a *more aggressive* prosecution of the war in Vietnam.

Just because sixties radicals were few in number doesn't mean they were irrelevant, however. In fact, during the 1960s, this radical minority gained a toehold in key American institutions, which they hijacked over the ensuing decades. Their biggest victory, of course, was America's defeat in Vietnam. Although they convinced gullible reporters to refer to them as "antiwar" activists, in fact much of the "antiwar" movement's leadership did not oppose the war as much as it wanted the other side to win. Today, our textbooks typically end their accounts of the Vietnam War with the withdrawal of American troops. This vindicates the radicals while conveniently failing to connect America's defeat in Vietnam to the resulting consequences: the torture of hundreds of thousands of people in Communist "reeducation" camps; the transformation of hundreds of thousands more into boat people and permanent refugees; and the spread of Communism to Laos as well as to Cambodia, where nearly two million people were killed by the Khmer Rouge.

In the course of mythologizing the sixties counterculture, the biographies of numerous sixties luminaries have been totally re-written. Supreme Court justice Earl Warren is no longer remembered for rounding up Japanese citizens into internment camps; rather, he is seen as an enlightened progressive thanks to the extremely liberal rulings issued by his court. Similarly, Malcolm X has been transformed into a noble civil rights activist and an ecumenical lover of people of all races and creeds. His real history as an anti-white racial separatist with a background in gay prostitution is not mentioned much anymore.

But, as John Adams said, "Facts are stubborn things." And this book aims to provide them, giving you the real story behind the Black Panthers,

Kennedy's 1960 "victory" over Nixon, the birth of rock 'n' roll, the advent of feminism, the Great Society, the moon landings, mod fashions, and many other subjects.

Here you'll learn how a small group of intellectuals—both in Washington and at our leading universities—worked in tandem with street thugs to undermine law, order, and family stability. It's a shocking but largely untold story that every American should know.

The truth may not be politically correct, but here it is.

Part I

❀ ❀ ❀ ❀ ❀

THE SOCIAL SIXTIES

Chapter One

THE STUDENT RADICALS: WHO THEY WERE AND WHICH GIRLS THEY WANTED

For former sixties radicals, the "student movement" has become a hallowed memory—the spark that gave rise to the New Left and set off a wider rebellion against American society. Enjoying exemptions from the military draft, student radicals were safely ensconced on their college campuses while the less-privileged cohort of their generation heeded the call to fight Communism in Vietnam. For their part, the radicals demonstrated their "courage" by fighting a different enemy back home, an enemy who, in their collective memory, was no less fearsome and brutal than the Viet Cong—their college administrators.

The activity of college radicals has been passed down as the archetypical experience of the 1960s. Through countless Hollywood movies, documentaries, and books, we encounter the image of radical students bravely occupying administrative buildings and defiantly marching on campus for one cause or another.

What's left unsaid is this: the radicals were a small minority on college campuses and were often held in disdain by their fellow students. The vast majority of college students in the 1960s were not political crusaders, but normal kids who spent their time going to classes, studying, dating, and pursuing other unremarkable activities. Many even joined ROTC, much to the radicals' chagrin. In sum, the radical students

Guess What?

- Most college campuses were not hotbeds of radicalism during the 1960s

- UC Berkeley's free speech movement was led by admitted Communists

- The Kent State shootings were provoked by widespread rioting and arson

1

comprised just a small minority of students, which made them an even smaller component of the sixties youth, and thus a minute part of sixties society overall. The fact that they have convinced younger generations that their saga is *the* quintessential experience of the 1960s is a testament to their own narcissism.

Leaders of the New Left: Marx would be proud

Who exactly comprised this minority of student agitators? Were they liberal idealists who wanted to make America into a better, more just, and more tolerant nation? This is what much of the mass media told the public at the time when students seized campus buildings or threw rocks at the police. The protestors were presented as heroic romantics.

But this was false. In fact, it's hard to think of a single group of people in the 1960s who were more hostile to openness and tolerance or more self-centered than the student leaders of the New Left.

Above all else, the student radicals were *politicians*—Communist politicians motivated by the immediate goals of thrills, sex, status, and power. Many were so-called "red diaper babies"—the children of American Communists who shared their parents' unrepentant belief that totalitarianism was superior to democracy. This includes many of the most famous and influential student agitators: Abbie Hoffman, Jerry Rubin, Bernardine Dohrn, Bettina Aptheker, Katherine Boudin, and Mark Rudd. Similarly, the lawyer representing the Chicago Seven—the conspirators responsible for the riots during the 1968 Democratic Convention—was long-time Communist Party lawyer William Kunstler.

Of course, most American college students at the time were not Communists. But Communists dominated the leadership of the sixties student radicals from the beginning, going all the way back to the free speech movement at Berkeley.

When Communists Repent

Many sixties leftist radicals have retained their anti-American outlook to this day. A 2001 photo of Bill Ayers, for example, shows the former Weatherman terrorist defiantly standing on an American flag. But a few of them eventually changed their tune. Chicago Seven member Jerry Rubin, for example, gave up his jeremiads against "the man" and became a rich Wall Street capitalist. David Horowitz underwent an even more striking transformation. The son of two die-hard Communists, Horowitz became one himself, going to work for the Black Panthers and editing the influential radical magazine *Ramparts*. Sickened by the Panthers' criminality and the refusal of his fellow leftwing radicals to denounce it, Horowitz became a Reagan-supporting conservative in the 1980s. He now attacks his former Communist allies with the same energy he previously devoted to denouncing American imperialism. He recounts his Communist upbringing and political transformation in his autobiography, *Radical Son*.

The Berkeley free speech movement: Free speech for us

The initial campus unrest of the 1960s was connected to the free speech movement at the University of California at Berkeley. The "movement" kicked off in 1964 as a protest against the school's ban on forming political organizations and raising money on campus for political causes. At the time, students could participate in politics off campus or join the College Democrats and College Republicans, but administrators believed that a public university should generally focus on academic work instead of politics, so they prohibited many political activities. The university was hardly a politically repressive environment, however. In fact, in

1963, just before the free speech movement began, university president Clark Kerr affirmed that even avowed Communists could give addresses to students and faculty.

Student leftist leaders at the time were particularly galvanized by two issues, both of which were the focus of propaganda campaigns by the American Communist Party (CPUSA). The first, civil rights, was the target of a long-standing Communist agitation campaign aimed at recruiting American blacks into the party. The second issue was the bourgeoning conflict in Vietnam; unsurprisingly, the CPUSA strongly supported its Communist Vietnamese comrades against the American soldiers opposing them.

Now There's a Tolerant, Open-Minded Person

"Some thirteen years later, in 1965, after I was married, living in Berkeley, and a member of the [Communist] party, my husband, who was also a Communist, tried to talk to me about the atrocities committed by Stalin. Almost reflexively, I shouted at him to stop and became hysterical."

—Bettina Aptheker[1]

At the time, the free speech movement's leaders claimed they were not Communists, but their denials rang hollow. *The* leader of the free speech movement was Bettina Aptheker, daughter of avowed Communist writer Herbert Aptheker and wife of Communist organizer Jack Kurzweil. Bettina came clean about her own membership in the Communist Party in November 1965 and later wrote about her Communism extensively in her memoirs, *Intimate Politics*.

The movement's second-leading figure, Mario Savio, comically claimed to be not a Marxist, but a "gentle Socialist." Nevertheless, his rhetoric throughout his whole life was filled with admiring references to Marxism, such as a speech in 1988 in which he complained that the Soviet leadership had begun "to acknowledge the truth in America's truth; our leaders, however, have not as yet begun publicly to acknowledge any truth in Marxist truth." Still, Savio conceded that one

American had seen the light of truth in Marxism: "Jesse Jackson is an exception, of course."[2]

Third among the free speech movement guides was Jackie Goldberg. Here is a description of this self-declared "progressive" from a 1965 California State Senate report:

> Jacqueline Goldberg, the sister of Arthur Goldberg, came from Los Angeles to attend the university at Berkeley. She soon became the head of U.C. Women for Peace, a front organization, and was its delegate to a Moscow meeting in 1963. She was also active in the American-Russian Institute at San Francisco, cited by the Attorney General of the United States as a Communist-dominated organization, and is now a member of the Policy Committee for the next World Communist Youth Festival which is scheduled to be held in Algeria. She was a member of both the executive and steering committees of FSM [the free speech movement], and was arrested during the invasion of Sproul Hall.[4]

Thus, the free speech movement, which is often portrayed today as a patriotic movement for student rights, was in fact led by two Communists and a "gentle Socialist." (It's unclear whether Aptheker and Goldberg considered themselves "gentle" Communists or just normal ones.)

The movement fully emerged on September 30, 1964, when Savio and a group of 150 protestors occupied Berkeley's main administration building, Sproul Hall, and stopped students and faculty from going to the dean's office. Savio riled up his student

Sure Sounds Like a Communist

"'From each according to his ability; to each according to his need.' My father could never hear the poetry in those words."

—Mario Savio, bemoaning his dad's stubborn refusal to appreciate the beauty of Communist slogans[3]

followers by accusing the school's overseers of doing the bidding of big business. When police arrived, Savio bit an officer's leg. He was suspended from the university along with seven other students, but throughout the following weeks Savio brazenly continued to lead protests on campus anyway.

The next day, a student named Jack Weinberg and his colleagues set up a table in front of Sproul Hall to promote civil rights. This was university property, and the students had no permission from the administration for their political activities. When police asked Weinberg to identify himself, he refused and was arrested.

For Aptheker, Savio, and Goldberg, this was the perfect pretext to provoke a major incident. Protesting students were dispatched to the scene to prevent a police car from driving Weinberg off to jail. As students blockaded the car with their bodies, Savio and others stood on the car's roof and made political speeches for more than a day. The timidity of the police emboldened the radicals, who claimed to act in the name of the students *en masse,* even though a crowd of opposing students gathered at the scene to condemn the protestors and voice support for the police.

Although Weinberg was ultimately released without charge, within days the incident led to the creation of the free speech movement steering committee, which included, at various times, Aptheker, Savio, and other bona fide Communists and socialists. With its semi-secret *ad hoc* membership behind it, the group dispatched 200 members to Sproul Hall on November 9 and again set up tables to pass out political pamphlets. The move was timed to pressure a meeting of the school's board of regents, which throughout these events showed a spineless unwillingness to enforce university rules on the protestors.

A Book You're Not Supposed to Read

Destructive Generation: Second Thoughts About the '60s by Peter Collier and David Horowitz (New York: Free Press, 1996).

In a rare show of backbone, however, the regents' meeting refused to give in to the protestors' demands to allow political activism on campus. So leftists turned out to protest once more, knowing quite well by now that punishment was unlikely. They declared a student strike on December 2 and, under the direction of the steering committee, more than a thousand students marched into Sproul and refused to leave, throwing the administrators out of their own buildings.

The school's chancellor, Edward Strong, distinguished himself as one of the few university administrators to insist that order be upheld on campus. He invited the California Highway Patrol to remove the protestors from Sproul, although the students were given yet *another* chance to avoid punishment if they would leave the building before the police arrived. Finally, the police entered and arrested more than 700 of the occupiers.

Everyone wondered if the school would at last punish the protestors—their actions blatantly violated school policies, and the disturbances were interfering with the rights of the majority of students who were more concerned with getting an education than with political protest. The University of California system's liberal and simpering president, Clark Kerr, clarified the matter on the following Monday when he told a mass meeting of students that *none* of the protestors would receive *any* punishment. As a result of this irresponsibility, the university abdicated its duty to act *in loco parentis* for its students, most of whom were minors, and encouraged student radicals to wreak havoc on other campuses.

And if the university president would not stand up to the protestors, why should the professors? After Kerr's announcement, the faculty voted on proposals to allow campus political activism using university facilities. Alarmed by the intimidating atmosphere growing around the radicals, faculty members Lewis Feuer and Nathan Glazer modestly suggested that this be limited to political activism that did not involve intimidation of students or threats of force and coercion. But by then events had gained their own momentum, propelled forward by the revolutionary willpower of the free speech movement leaders. Reasonable concerns to protect students from intimidation were swept away, and the faculty rejected Feuer and Glazer's proposal. Then, on January 2, 1965, the regents fired Chancellor Strong, who had invited the police to remove the Sproul Hall trespassers, and replaced him with Martin Meyerson, a free speech movement supporter who finally opened up the Berkeley campus to political activities.

Encountering very little resistance, a small group of Communist-led activists had exploited a few events that they themselves had largely manufactured and effectively seized control of a major American university. Many Californians were repulsed by the petulant protests of kids whose education was being subsidized by the state's taxpayers. In 1966, Californians elected Ronald Reagan—who had condemned the paralyzed inaction of Berkeley administrators—governor of their state. A decade later, former San Francisco State president S. I. Hayakawa would be elected to the United States Senate from California as a conservative Republican, largely on the fame he had won as an opponent of the student radicals in the late 1960s and early 1970s.

What is most remarkable about the Berkeley takeover, perhaps, is how simple it was. The Berkeley radicals had demonstrated to the whole nation that university administrators could easily be intimidated and usurped. And inevitably their model of "direct action" was followed on many other campuses nationwide. From that point on, America's universities became the main base of operations for the New Left.

Students for a Democratic Society: From radicalism to terrorism

While the free speech movement disguised its leaders' Communist sympathies, other student organizations openly proclaimed them. The most influential of these Marxist groups was Students for a Democratic Society (SDS), founded in Ann Arbor, Michigan, in 1960. Originally a proponent of Swedish-style democratic socialism, the group became increasingly militant in the mid-to-late 1960s as the Vietnam War heated up. It quickly became the locus of the student antiwar movement.

By 1969, the SDS had become an openly Communist organization with almost 70,000 members.[5] Its leaders traveled on solidarity missions to Communist countries. In 1967, for example, SDS co-founder Tom Hayden led a group of forty-one activists on a trip to Czechoslovakia to express solidarity with North Vietnam and the Viet Cong. By 1970, SDS

The "Antiwar" Movement

One of the great gifts the media gave the radical students of the 1960s was to refer to them during the Vietnam War as part of an "antiwar movement." While there were undoubtedly some leftists who were genuine pacifists, many were motivated by a different concern: college students were given deferments from military conscription, and they hoped to end the war before they finished college and became eligible for the draft. That it was the fear of being drafted above all else that spurred student radicalism is made clear by the abrupt decline in campus protests after President Nixon ended the draft in 1973.

Furthermore, many of the "antiwar" protestors were not actually "antiwar" at all; they just supported the other side, as shown by the popular "antiwar" chant, "Ho, Ho, Ho Chi Minh. NLF is gonna win." This was a tribute to Communist North Vietnamese leader Ho Chi Minh and his brutal armed force in South Vietnam, the National Liberation Front, also known as the Viet Cong.

had helped more than a thousand college students move to Cuba to assist Castro's revolution. The gullible students were put to work harvesting sugar by day and studying Marxism-Leninism by night.[6]

Understandably, these kinds of pro-Communist stunts attracted a lot of media attention, creating the misperception that college campuses were teeming with leftwing radicals. The truth, however, is that the activists were a noisy, intimidating minority. Throughout the 1960s, more college students classified themselves as conservative than anything else. College groups like the Young Republicans and Young Americans for Freedom enjoyed robust membership, though their reluctance to occupy campus buildings, lead riots, or embrace Communist leaders meant that they were overshadowed in the media by their leftwing counterparts. What's more, conservative stalwart Barry Goldwater was the most requested campus speaker in the early 1960s, more requested than Malcolm X, Tom Hayden, or Huey Newton.[7]

The SDS, however, developed an attention-grabbing agenda that came out foursquare in support of America's wartime enemies in Vietnam. It wrapped this agenda in a cloak of presumptuous, hypocritical pseudo-morality, condemning American troops as baby-killers and denouncing America as racist and imperialistic. These assertions were ironic in light of the brutality and racism exhibited by the Vietnamese Communists, who terrorized and murdered their political opponents in the South, herded ethnic Chinese into concentration camps, and fought tenaciously to subjugate their neighbors in Laos and Cambodia.

SDS leaders distinguished themselves from their Vietnamese Communist idols in one important respect, however. Whereas the Viet Cong tended to be ascetics, if only by necessity, many SDS leaders were hedonists as well as Communists. They encouraged the breaking of sexual norms like chastity and monogamy as revolutionary and heroic acts. The "movement heavies," as SDS leaders were known, were treated like rock stars by militant girls, who were encouraged to demonstrate their revolutionary credentials by sleeping with such SDS honchos as Mark Rudd and John Jacobs. As a male delegate at SDS's 1965 convention noted, women in the group "made peanut butter, waited on tables, cleaned up, got laid. That was their role." A woman who criticized this view from the convention floor was shouted down by a man's insistence that "she just needs a good screw."[8]

Almost from its inception, the SDS was riven by infighting, as commonly occurs in extremist groups. And by 1966 it had already begun splintering into two factions. The first, the Revolutionary Youth Movement (RYM), was a Trotskyite, pro-Cuban group. Rejecting the possibility of white industrial workers leading a Communist revolution in America, the RYM looked for leadership to racial gangs like the Black Panther Party and the Young Lords.

Its rival faction was called Progressive Labor (PL), a mostly humorless cohort of committed Maoists who wanted to imitate China's murderous Cultural Revolution in the streets of America. Unlike RYM members, who often had long hair and smoked pot, PL members were instructed to keep their hair short and dress respectably so as not to alienate industrial workers, whom they hoped to recruit to the cause of the revolution. At SDS meetings, PL members would routinely read out the latest installments from the *Peking Daily*, the English-language version of the official voice of the Communist Chinese Party. Displays such as these provoked ridicule from the Beatles, who sang in their tune *Revolution*, "But if you go carrying pictures of Chairman Mao/You ain't going to make it with anyone anyhow."

Despite their differences, both SDS factions sought to undermine the U.S. war effort, help the Viet Cong to win, and spark a Communist revolution at home. One early and influential SDS member, Dotson Rader, admitted later that the conflicts within SDS did not stem from ideological

SDS Resurrected?

After disappearing from the scene for nearly forty years, in 2006 a group of teenage activists teamed up with some former SDS members to try to resurrect the organization. Meeting with some success, they now claim to have 120 active chapters. The group, however, has encountered some problems.

First, at a time when the Soviet Union has collapsed and even Vietnam is adopting capitalism, a pro-Communist student group risks not being taken seriously. So what exactly does the reborn SDS stand for? The organization unleashed an extremely long mission statement filled with stilted political jargon. Combining warmed-over socialism with modern political correctness, the statement pledges to "target structures of domination," "build powerful diverse movements for change," and combat "systems of white supremacy, patriarchy, capitalism, imperialism, heterosexism, transphobia, and the many other forms of oppression."[9]

Good luck with that.

Second, the SDS tarnished itself by participating in the ill-fated, three-day student occupation of a cafeteria at New York University in early 2009. After putting forward a litany of unrelated demands ranging from transparency in the school budget to the provision of supplies to the Gaza Strip's Islamic University, the student rebels were abruptly ejected by the police after three days, with eighteen students getting suspended.[10] On the internet, a popular video clip showed security officers easily pushing aside a flimsy barricade while the would-be insurgents pathetically pleaded, "Excuse me, you may not come in here, this is a student free space." The ignominious end to the ordeal did little to burnish the neo-SDS's reputation as a re-forged band of fearless radicals. As one blogger commented, "To be this far over the line into self-parody and yet somehow oblivious to it is hard to fathom; it feels like satire, but it isn't."[11]

differences so much as from "opportunism and youth and careerist ambitions and romanticism and taste for power."[12]

Tension between the two factions came to a head at SDS's 1969 national convention in Chicago. PL members from across the country showed up in huge numbers with the intention of voting out the RYM leadership and taking control. But when faced with defeat, Bernardine Dohrn, Mike Klonsky, and other RYM leaders formed a rump group in an auditorium next door, then returned to announce they were dismissing all the PL members, who numbered over a thousand.

The RYM leaders then proclaimed that the SDS would become a new group called the Weatherman—a name taken from the Bob Dylan lyric, "You don't need a weatherman to tell which way the wind blows." The Weatherman took an even more radical form than the SDS, constituting itself as a terrorist group that became known primarily for its bombing spree against domestic military and political targets. On one occasion, three Weatherman terrorists accidentally killed themselves when their own bomb exploded in a townhouse in New York's Greenwich Village. The bomb was meant to be used to kill U.S. soldiers in a planned attack on the army base at Fort Dix, New Jersey.

The Weatherman took its commitment to violence to a near-comical extreme. The group's communiqués declared that "revolutionary violence is the only way" to destroy the system of "Amerikan [sic] injustice."[13] A favorite slogan of the group, popularized by Bill Ayers, now famous as a friend of Barack Obama's and as a professor of education, was "Bring the revolution home, kill your parents." Another Weatherman slogan was "Smash Monogamy!" At a "war council" in Flint, Michigan, Weatherman leader Bernardine Dohrn held her hand up and divided her fingers into what she called a "fork salute." The gesture celebrated the murder of actress Sharon Tate and her friends by the deranged followers of cult leader Charles Manson. As Dohrn exclaimed, "Dig it! First they killed those pigs, then they ate dinner in the same room with them. They even shoved a fork into the victim's stomach. Wild!"[14]

There was not much need for SDS anymore once it had spawned the ultra-radical Weatherman. At that point SDS died out, replaced entirely by its terrorist successor. After presiding over a series of bombings, the Weatherman itself splintered into various factions and successor groups. The most notorious of these, the May 19 Communist Coalition, participated in the 1981 New York Brinks armored car robbery, during which two police officers and a security guard were murdered. Eventually, nearly all the Weatherman leaders surrendered to the authorities or were captured.

Kent State: The untold story

Aside from the Vietnam War, it would be hard to think of anything that has obsessed the New Left as much as the Kent State shootings. Although it occurred in May 1970, the incident is now remembered as one of the quintessential events of the 1960s. It was famously memorialized in the Crosby, Stills, Nash & Young tune, "Four Dead in Ohio," and in dozens of other songs by performers including the Steve Miller Band, Bruce Springsteen, the Beach Boys, Joe Walsh, Holly Near, the founders of Devo, Dave Brubeck, and Jon Anderson of Yes. Additionally, there are poems commemorating the event by Allen Ginsberg and Yevgeny Yevtushenko, numerous sculptures (including one by famed realist George Segal), five documentaries, and at least three theatrical or network television films. All these memorials tell the same story: vicious National Guardsmen, without provocation, opened fire on peaceful "antiwar" protestors.

But that's not what really happened.

Most accounts of the shootings only look at Kent State, and thus conveniently omit the wider context of the times; namely, that the shootings

How Barack Obama Is Mixed Up in All This

Bill Ayers was one of the Weatherman's most notorious terrorists. For Ayers, who joined the SDS early on and rapidly rose to leadership posts, the SDS provided an arena for competing over "sexual conquests, street fighting ability, and eventually the ability to talk tough."[15] Indeed, as an SDS "heavy," Ayers had his share of lovers, including Diana Oughton, who was one of those killed in the Weatherman's Greenwich Village townhouse explosion. He eventually married SDS beauty Bernardine Dohrn.

After the group was founded, Ayers was named its education secretary and was chosen as one of five central committee members. During his time as a Weatherman, Ayers, by his own admission, participated in bombings of the New York City Police Headquarters, the United States Capitol, and the Pentagon, among other targets. Having avoided conviction thanks to legal technicalities, he is unrepentant about his past crimes, telling the *New York Times* in 2001, "I don't regret setting bombs."[16]

Along with Dohrn, Ayers became an early backer of Barack Obama, hosting the first fundraiser for Obama when he was running for the Illinois State Senate in 1995. Obama and Ayers served together as board members of the leftwing Woods Hole Foundation, and Obama also served as board chairman of the Chicago Annenberg Challenge, a radical education foundation founded by Ayers. During his presidential campaign Obama described Ayers as just "a guy who lived in my neighborhood." Ayers dutifully kept quiet about their relationship during Obama's campaign, but after Obama's victory Ayers wrote that he and Obama were "family friends."[17]

were preceded by a spate of rioting and violence by agitators at other universities, including UC Berkeley, Columbia, and Harvard. Most famously, Cornell's Willard Straight Hall was taken over by black power activists who later had guns smuggled into the building. Although it is not noted by pop singers or filmmakers, these leftist radicals often left a trail of mayhem. At the University of Wisconsin at Madison, for example, researcher Robert Fassnacht was murdered by "antiwar" student terrorists who bombed the school's Sterling Hall Army Math Research Center.

Unrest first hit Kent State in April 1969, when Columbia SDS leader Mark Rudd gave a speech on campus.[18] Rudd's address was a standard-issue tirade that was strong on demagogy and short on love or pacifism. He called for students to fight to shut down the school's ROTC program, its crime labs, and its law enforcement training classes.

Over the next year, a faction of radical Kent State students took up Rudd's call, issuing a manifesto echoing his demands. Among the principal leaders was self-professed Communist Robert Franklin.[19] The agitators "occupied" university buildings by breaking in through locked doors and windows. Meeting little resistance from school authorities, they became increasingly fanatical, and their actions encouraged extremism from other student groups. The Black United Students, for example, called for achieving their goals "by any means necessary"—a clear indication that violence was an option.[20]

By Friday, May 1, 1970, the situation at Kent State was spinning completely out of control. That day, students buried a copy of the Constitution and then publicly burned a draft card. A mob set fire to the school's Air Force ROTC building, while also torching an American flag. A student who tried to photograph the event was beaten and robbed of his camera. When fire marshals arrived to stop the blaze, the gang of arsonists attacked them and stole their hoses. The building burned into the evening.[21]

Worse was to come. That night students poured into the center of the town, starting more fires. They overwhelmed the police, who were unwilling to use their guns, and beat numerous cops as well as the town's mayor. Local officials began asking the governor to declare a state of emergency.

Still unpunished, the student mob went further the following day. Having succeeded in torching the Air Force ROTC building with impunity, it set fire to the Kent State president's building. Then the radicals headed back downtown and began smashing up stores. The disorder rapidly spread, eventually involving around two thousand people. Rock-throwing mobs roamed the town. At a nearby airstrip, a truck was stolen, six planes were attacked, and another fire was started.[22]

Behind this violence was a small group of hard-core agitators whose demands ran the gamut from ending the draft to abolishing tuition.

That Monday morning National Guard troops arrived to re-take the campus from the looters and arsonists. The ringleaders had organized a bigger group of students around themselves, essentially using them as human shields. After ordering the students to leave, the Guardsmen began moving toward the crowd to disperse it. Between ten and fifty students then began throwing rocks at the Guardsmen, and some students reportedly attempted to throw a parking meter off a building roof at the troops.[23] Worse, the Guardsmen became caught behind the chain-link fence of a practice football facility. They were trapped and under attack.

Then something quite unexpected happened. Eyewitnesses reported that a student named Terry Norman pulled out a gun and pistol-whipped another student. He then pointed the gun at the Guardsmen and started running toward them.[24] The Guardsmen opened fire, killing four students.

Leftwing activists have concocted the farfetched conspiracy theory that Norman was really an FBI agent planted at the scene by the government.

As evidence, they note that Norman, who was a professional photographer, had taken pictures for the FBI of a neo-Nazi rally in a nearby town.[26] This indeed appears to be the case. But that's hardly evidence that Norman was at Kent State as a government plant. The Justice Department and the FBI repeatedly investigated this claim, going over 8,000 pages of FBI files and interviewing many witnesses. Over one hundred agents were involved in just one of the investigations, and the Justice Department's review was conducted under the aegis of liberal icon and Nixon antagonist Elliot Richardson.[27] There were also two federal trials of the Guardsmen, one criminal and one civil, both resulting in the dismissal of

Oops, Nevermind

During the 1960s, West Germany had a similar incident to the Kent State shooting. In 1967, a West German police officer shot and killed a university student, Benno Ohnesorg, during a leftwing protest. The killing sparked widespread outrage and was frequently cited as justification for terrorist attacks by German leftist groups like the Second of June Movement, which was named after the date of Ohnesorg's death, and the Red Army Faction. Ohnesorg's death also helped to consolidate a radical student protest movement that pushed German politics well to the left.

As was the case at Kent State, however, there was more to the situation than met the eye. In 2009 researchers discovered that the policeman who shot Ohnesorg was an agent of the Stasi, the secret police of Communist East Germany. The far left in Germany spent over thirty years demonizing the officer, Karl-Heinz Kurras, as a fascist murderer, when it turns out he was actually on their side all along.[25]

all charges.[28] There was even a further investigation of Norman's involvement prompted by a public request from Democratic senator Birch Bayh. None of these inquiries has ever provided any evidence that Norman was a secret government agent.

The tragic deaths at Kent State included students who were innocent bystanders uninvolved in the rioting. But in the rush to proclaim the victims as martyrs for the New Left, the arson, looting, and violence of the "antiwar" agitators has been all but erased from history. There surely was no mention of the riots in "Four Dead in Ohio"—as if the "tin soldier" Guardsmen opened fire totally unprovoked, just because they were the evil representatives of an immoral government. Needless to say, if there had been no rioting, the National Guard would not have been called, and the four students would not have been slain.

The radicals go to grad school and take over the faculty

Student radicals across the country quickly realized that school administrators were easily intimidated by campus disruptions or even the mere threat of student unrest. Weak-kneed administrators capitulated to one radical demand after another, eventually ceding control of much of their curriculum to the radicals, who insisted on providing overtly politicized courses in ethnic studies, women's studies, gay studies, "whiteness" studies, and the like.

The radicals soon took over faculty departments and the university administrations themselves. By hiring other radicals and excluding everyone else, the original sixties radicals strengthened and transformed their position among faculties and administrations from being an obnoxious minority to being an obnoxious majority. Having failed to take over the United States government, they took academia as a consolation prize.

There is a long list of radicals who have made the transition from the sixties student Left to the tenured Left today. Here is just a small sample:

- **Bill Ayers** (University of Illinois, Chicago). After years as a Weatherman terrorist and fugitive, Ayers seems to have become dissatisfied with the paltry 401(k) plan available to domestic bombers. Academia not only offered Ayers much better financial benefits, but it also enabled him to continue his radical politics. He is now a tenured education professor and an influential advocate of teaching "social justice."

- **Bettina Aptheker** (University of California, Santa Cruz). The former leader of Berkeley's free speech movement and Communist Party member earned a Ph.D. in something called "History of Consciousness." She later declared herself a lesbian and found employment as a professor of feminist studies, insisting to students that lesbianism is "the highest stage of feminism."[29] In 2006 she caused some controversy on the Left when she published a memoir accusing her late father, Herbert Aptheker, of sexually molesting her for a period of ten years. Angered that Aptheker would soil the reputation of her father, a committed Communist and hero to the New Left, some of Aptheker's colleagues voiced doubts about her allegations, which she said resulted from a process of recovered memories.

- **H. Bruce Franklin** (Rutgers University). Franklin was co-founder in 1969 of a group called the Bay Area Revolutionary Union, recruiting hundreds of armed followers for the cause of Maoist revolution. In 1971 he formed a new body called Venceremos that promoted the ideas of Fidel Castro. Franklin also admired other Communist mass murderers such as Joseph Stalin, whom Franklin lauded as "certainly one of the greatest revolutionary figures." In 1972 Franklin was fired from his teaching position at Stanford for inciting a riot, though he rebounded to receive an endowed, tenured position as an English professor at Rutgers. [30]

- **José Angel Gutiérrez** (University of Texas, Arlington). In 1967 Gutierrez took time off from his graduate studies to found the Mexican American Youth Organization (MAYO), a militant nationalist Chicano organization. He later created

Holding onto Those Draft Deferments

One of the key events contributing to academia's long-term transformation was the provision of student deferments during the Vietnam War. The most immediate consequence of student deferments was grade inflation. Sympathizing with antiwar students, liberal professors made sure they would get at least a 2.0 grade point average—the minimum necessary to maintain their deferment. As a result, academic standards quickly degraded. Between 1967 and 2002, the average grade at all colleges and universities jumped by more than .6 on a 4.0 scale. Roughly half this rise appeared just between 1967 and 1972. Where once a "gentleman's C" signified a competent mediocrity at a prestigious college, it soon became a mark close to failure. At both Harvard and Yale the average grade is now well above a B, and more than 70 percent of all grades are A's or B's.[33]

A large number of student radicals went on to graduate school in order to maintain their deferments. After completing a higher degree, it made good career sense for them to become professors and adopt the comfortable, bourgeois lifestyle they had spent the previous decade denouncing. Many of these rebels can still be found on college campuses, driving minivans with "fight the power" bumper stickers.

La Raza Unida, a group that aims to split several south-western states from the United States and turn them into a separate Chicano nation. Gutierrez is a law professor who claims that civil rights are just "law made by white men to oppress all of us of color." As for his ultimate agenda, Gutierrez insists that "we have got to eliminate the *gringo*, and what I mean by that is that if worst comes to the worst, we have got to kill him." After all, Gutierrez says, "Our devil has pale skin and blue eyes."[31]

- **Tom Hayden** (Occidental College). A former SDS president, Hayden took numerous solidarity trips to Communist North Vietnam during the Vietnam War. He does not seem to have mellowed in his old age, using his professorship to promote the cause of Marxist guerrillas in Mexico and to encourage active-duty U.S. troops to desert and flee to Canada.[32] Still, Hayden may have already done his penance: he spent seventeen years married to Jane Fonda.

- **Angela Davis** (University of California, Santa Cruz). A former Communist Party USA vice presidential candidate, Davis was involved with the Black Panthers and once appeared on the FBI's Ten Most Wanted List in connection with a fatal shooting during a Black Panther prison break. She lived for some time in Castro's Cuba, and is now a tenured professor of "History of Consciousness" and an "advocate of prison abolition."[34]

- **Ron Karenga** (California State University, Long Beach). Karenga was a black nationalist leader as a doctoral student at UCLA in the mid-1960s. He founded the radical group Organization US (United Slaves) and is best known for inventing the holiday of Kwanzaa in 1966 as a black nationalist alternative to Christmas. After serving jail time for severely beating two women, Karenga went on to become chairman of the Black Studies Department at CSU Long Beach and author of a seminal black studies textbook, *Introduction to Black Studies*, a radical attack on white society.[35]

- **Orville Schell** (University of Southern California). Schell co-founded the Pacific News Service in 1969 to provide anti-American reporting on the war in Vietnam. After his appointment as dean of the Berkeley Journalism School, Schell seeded the school with radical friends and acquaintances, turning the school into a hotbed of leftwing radicalism.[36]

The examples of Karenga and Schell in particular get to the wider problem. It isn't just that 1960s-era leftists teach hatred and contempt for capitalism, America, white people, and the rule of law, but that they hire their allies to teach this, too—and refuse to hire those who don't share their beliefs. Ironically, when the 1960s began, many teachers had to take oaths affirming they were not Communists; now many are tenured Communists and won't permit conservatives, independents, libertarians, or even moderate liberals the job opportunities they themselves received.

The decline and fall of the American university

The ascendency of sixties radicals in academia transformed the American university's core mission. While academics had previously dedicated themselves to the "disinterested pursuit of knowledge," the goal of the 1960s cohort was to spread "social justice"—a clever euphemism that simply means to struggle for a leftwing political agenda. Believing that no sphere was off limits to politics, the sixties radicals politicized academic work and hiring decisions; after all, to quote a famous sixties slogan, even "the personal is political."

I Don't Think They Offered These Classes Before the 1960s

In 2007 the Young America's Foundation published the "Top 10 Most Bizarre and Politically Correct College Courses":

10. Nonviolent Responses to Terrorism

9. American Dreams/American Realities

8. Cyberfeminism

7. Mail Order Brides: Understanding the Philippines in Southeast Asian Context

6. Whiteness: The Other Side of Racism

5. Blackness

4. Adultery Novel

3. Taking Marx Seriously

2. Queer Musicology

1. The Phallus[37]

As a result, the guiding principle at American universities is now multiculturalism, a doctrine that rejects the traditional American notion of the melting pot. Instead of a unified American culture, multiculturalists encourage immigrants to retain their native cultures in order to bring about "diversity"—a magical condition in which the interaction of many different cultures creates some ill-defined state of nirvana removed from traditional Western civilization. Multiculturalism spread alongside a stifling code of political correctness, which holds that certain "victimized" identity groups—particularly gays, women, and any non-white racial or ethnic group—should never be subject to criticism or even jokes. To enforce this orthodoxy, college administrators promulgated an Orwellian system of speech codes—an ironic outcome for a group that once claimed to be part of a "free speech" movement.

The robust employment of sixties radicals is largely responsible for the expansion of the least serious and substantive college departments, so-called fields like ethnic studies, critical legal theory, and sociology. Unsurprisingly, these departments are largely dominated by leftwing teacher-activists. In fact, exhaustive studies by Everett Carll Ladd Jr. and Seymour Martin Lipset, professors at the University of Connecticut and Harvard, respectively, found an inverse correlation between professors' political radicalism and the amount of hard science in their area of study.

Those professors in "soft" research fields like sociology are most likely to be far left, while those in more substantive disciplines like chemistry, biology, and agriculture are the least likely to harbor anti-capitalist views.

Furthermore, Ladd and Lipset found that medical school professors were more than twice as likely as sociology professors to have been among the academic minority to have voted for Nixon over McGovern, while engineering professors were more than three times as likely to have done so. Sociology and social psychology professors, in contrast, were the most likely to be supportive of student violence on campus.[38] Since there are few practical jobs for specialists in "queer theory" or "ethnic studies," it is clear enough that these departments exist primarily to find work for radicals and to give them a place to air their views.

From their comfortable professorships and deanships, sixties radicals promote their old agenda—revolution. Their pretensions have become more modest, however, since their youthful heyday when they sought to overthrow the United States government and all of capitalism. They now work toward overthrowing traditional academic standards and curricula and replacing them with various politicized theories that reflect their own worldview.

A Book You're Not Supposed to Read

Tenured Radicals: How Politics Has Corrupted Our Higher Education by Roger Kimball (New York: Harper and Row, 1990).

This is most evident in English departments, where the adherents of the New Left launched an all-out attack on the Western literary canon. Denounced as oppressive dead white males, literary greats like Shakespeare and Faulkner were purged from many syllabi.

It was during the 1960s that literary theorist Jacques Derrida became particularly influential among leftwing intellectuals. A consistent supporter of leftwing political causes such as Palestinian nationalism and, later, "justice" for convicted cop killer and death row inmate Mumia Abu-Jamal, Derrida wrote in his native French, adopting a strange style that was deliberately obscure and indecipherable.

His basic idea was clear enough, though: it was an attack on the entire concept of language, which Derrida argued is clouded by the effects of our own biases, racism, sexism, and "ethnocentrism." In Derrida's viewpoint, books and other literature have no inherent meaning, since they can be interpreted in conflicting ways, regardless of the author's intent. Derrida's theory, which he called deconstructionism, spread quickly among the new cohort of English professors, who were intrigued by the revolutionary implications of a single nihilistic theory that could overthrow all the accumulated knowledge in their field.

Derrida's critics noted that his theory could be invoked to justify crimes or any other act of misbehavior—after all, how can anyone's actions be judged, since a judgment must be expressed through language, which will be distorted by the speaker's own prejudices? This "who-are-you-to-judge" kind of nihilism became particularly useful to Derrida when he defended his principal American acolyte, the late Yale Professor Paul de Man. De Man was revealed to have covered up an earlier life as a virulently anti-Semitic Nazi journalist and collaborator in wartime Belgium, as well as a bigamist who had abandoned his wife and children to create a new life in America as a liberal academic.[39]

In any event, a cult developed around Derrida by the end of the 1960s, spawning an international cohort of Derrida disciples that came to control the English and literature faculties at Yale, Duke, and dozens of other schools. What's more, off-shoot brands of deconstructionist philosophy soon emerged in seemingly unrelated fields. In law, for example, a school of Marxist deconstructionist thinking appeared called Critical Legal Studies. Unsurprisingly, these practitioners argue that the Western legal code is really a racist rationalization of economic tyranny.

Radicals never were a majority or anything close to it on American college campuses in the 1960s. But one of the striking—and destructive—legacies of the 1960s is that this radical minority has come to dominate American higher education, using this privileged platform to indoctrinate generations of students in hateful, corrosive, and absurd ideologies. The old tweed-jacketed absentminded professor who loved the pursuit of knowledge is today, more often than not, an anachronism, replaced by a tenured radical whose heroes aren't Shakespeare and Jane Austen, Goethe and George Washington, Beethoven and Brahms, but Stalin and Mao, Castro and Che, Mapplethorpe and Lennon (and Lenin too).

Chapter Two

THE SEXUAL REVOLUTION AND THE START OF FEMINISM: WHERE'D MOM AND POP GO?

During the 1960s Americans finally discovered sex and got over their bourgeois hang-ups, right? Well, no.

Like so much about the sixties, the idea that a sexual revolution took place and that the majority of American young people suddenly took up "free love" is a myth. There was a rise in premarital sex during the 1960s, to be sure, but this was merely a continuation of a trend that had started much earlier and would not really take off until the 1970s. Twenty-three percent of 18-year-old girls reported having premarital sex in 1961 and 29 percent in 1970, but the number jumps to 54 percent by 1982, according to a University of Chicago study.[1]

Much greater changes in sexual behavior took place in the 1920s and 1940s than in the 1960s. In fact, even the term "sexual revolution" was an old one by the 1960s, having been introduced decades earlier by Sigmund Freud's nutty follower, Wilhelm Reich. Sexual mores in America had been gradually and steadily liberalizing since the 1890s, when large numbers of people began migrating from farms and small towns into major metropolises. Red light districts flourished in most major American cities by the turn of the century, and during the Jazz Age a generation later, the "flapper"—a fast and loose woman, often having been "ruined" in the back seat of a car—had become a literary cliché. *Playboy* first appeared on the shelves of American stores in 1953.

Guess What?

- The sexual revolution started in 1890, not 1960

- Nineteenth-century women's rights activists warned against legalizing abortion

- The 1960s feminist movement was started by moderate liberals and hijacked by radicals

So before the 1960s America was not as straitlaced as is commonly assumed, and yet sexual promiscuity was not nearly as widespread in the 1960s as is commonly believed. For all the liberalizing of sexual mores over the twentieth century, America remained socially conservative. The early 1960s in particular was characterized by sexual restraint even on college campuses. University administrators would not allow boys in girls' college dorm rooms after dark, and single-sex education was far more common than today, including at elite schools such as Princeton, Yale, Vassar, and Columbia. Even in the Ivy League, as Harvard men dating Radcliffe coeds in the mid-1960s could have told you, the vast majority of female students were committed to "saving themselves for marriage." Except in a few heady places like Haight-Ashbury, things weren't so wild. Almost no one had heard of co-ed dorms, and co-ed bathrooms were decades away.

While sexual mores during the 1960s gradually loosened, continuing the trend of the previous seven decades, a number of events served to make sexual issues a more common topic of public discussion. While the advent of the birth control pill in 1960 gets a lot of attention, a less well-remembered factor is that homosexuality first became a political issue in the 1960s. Liberal courts were often unwilling to enforce obscenity charges, which opened up space for the publication of gay-themed books like John Rechy's 1963 novel *City of Night*, a celebration of gay promiscuity in Los Angeles, and plays like Mart Crowley's 1968 *The Boys in the Band*. In 1969 gays fought against police officers who raided a gay bar in Greenwich Village, commencing the Stonewall Riots and sparking the modern gay rights movement. Furthermore, the well-publicized affairs of some of the biggest Hollywood celebrities, including Cary Grant, Elizabeth Taylor, Lana Turner, Marilyn Monroe, and Mickey Rooney, all became fodder for public conversation.

The 1960s also witnessed a dramatic rise in the popularity of Freudian psychoanalysis among university professors and other intellectuals.

Freud's popularity ushered in a more open discussion of sex based on the dubious theory that people should have sex more freely and openly because sexual inhibition causes neuroticism and hysteria—which was ironic given that Freud himself believed that civilization was based on the necessity of repressing many sexual urges and other compulsions. A similar exhortation to sexual promiscuity was voiced by adherents of British philosopher Bertrand Russell, whose promotion of "free love" became fashionable among academics in the 1960s, partly thanks to Russell's outspoken opposition to the Vietnam War and nuclear deterrence (which he had formerly supported; he had even, earlier, advocated a first strike against the Soviet Union). A perpetual philanderer, Russell had argued as far back as the 1920s for looser concepts of sexual morality and for the social acceptance of sex outside of marriage.

Another element pushing sex into the public discourse was the reorientation of *Cosmopolitan*, a family and literary magazine dating back to the 1800s. In 1965 it came under the editorship of Helen Gurley Brown, author of the bestselling book *Sex and the Single Girl*, a kind of how-to manual for young, single women to lead sexually satisfying lives. Brown, who would remain *Cosmopolitan* editor in chief for more than thirty years, turned the magazine into a low-brow, sex-focused glossy geared toward young women. She encouraged these women to enjoy lots of sex with multiple partners (including married men), avoid marrying young or having children, and to amuse themselves by sexually teasing men.[2]

Cosmo proffered a rather demeaning view of men, and men were encouraged to have a similarly degrading attitude toward women at

No Longer in Vogue

After enjoying widespread acclaim among "intellectuals" during the sixties, Freud has become *persona non grata* at numerous universities today. Many professors now view his politically-incorrect postulations—such as young girls suffering from "penis envy"—as being offensive to women.

Playboy Clubs, the first of which opened its doors in 1960. Club members, served by attractive waitresses in bunny outfits, were treated to a fantasy of busty, submissive women inclined toward no-strings-attached sex.

What all these trends added up to was this: during the 1960s, sexual permissiveness spread much more slowly than did the *encouragement* of permissiveness by opinion-setters. Sex became a bigger part of popular culture, leading people to believe that sexual morals had become looser than they really were. Although the swingers' movie *Bob & Carol & Ted & Alice* is considered a classic comedy that captures the supposedly licentious mood of the sixties, actual orgies, mate-swapping, and "key parties" are really all phenomena of the 1970s. The vaunted "sexual revolution" for which sixties radicals take credit is really just another sixties myth, though its later triumph must be considered one of their greatest and most harmful legacies, resulting as it has in astronomically higher rates of sexual disease, divorce, abortion, single-parent households, childlessness, and even loneliness, as more people live alone now than ever before.

Strange Beginnings

A New York Playboy Club was the unlikely launching point for the career of professional feminist Gloria Steinem, who wrote an exposé of her employment as a Playboy Club bunny.

The advent of feminism

The beginning of the feminist movement may have been one of the most significant phenomena of the 1960s, yet it is also one of the most misunderstood. The confusion arises principally because what we label feminism today is really composed of two opposing movements lumped together in one category. Just as the term "civil rights movement" now encompasses both the integrationist strand led by Martin Luther King Jr., and the opposing black separatist movement led by the likes of Malcolm X, two clashing strains of feminism are marked by a common term.

The leaders of feminism's liberal and radical wings, Betty Friedan and Gloria Steinem, respectively, had some superficial similarities in their backgrounds—both grew up in the Midwest, graduated with honors from Smith College, and had worked as freelance journalists. In terms of temperament and political outlook, however, they were little, if anything, alike.

The late Betty Friedan was a woman of powerful intellect and writing talent, if a monster of self-absorption and egotism. Homely, status-obsessed, and bent on fame, her writing tends toward overstatement, and

How to Be a Real Liberated Woman: Sleep Around, then Marry a Millionaire

Helen Gurley Brown held herself out as the quintessential "Cosmo girl," having stayed single until she was thirty-seven. Then, she gloated, she bagged a wealthy movie producer and ended up with "two Mercedes-Benzes, one hundred acres of virgin forest near San Francisco, a Mediterranean house overlooking the Pacific, a full time maid and the good life."[3]

her personality was caustic, divisive, and histrionic. Steinem is quite the opposite—conciliatory, calm, and exceptionally beautiful as a young woman. More inclined to promote others than herself, Steinem is a modest women who has suffered from low self-esteem, as evidenced in her book, *Revolution from Within*. Steinem makes few enemies and is fondly remembered by her former lovers, while many people who knew Friedan came to detest her.[4]

Based on these personality traits, one might assume that Steinem represented the moderate vision of feminism and Friedan the radical one. But this would be wrong—utterly and completely wrong. Complaisant and agreeable as Steinem's television personality may be, she and her many allies were hijackers, people who arrived late on a ship that they took over and sent in a new direction, one far from the craft's stated destination.

Friedan was the builder of the original ship of American feminism. The vessel she constructed was based on theories propounded by psychologist Abraham Maslow in the 1930s. Maslow's argument was rather straightforward: once basic human requirements like food and shelter were met, people would seek creative outlets to express their intrinsic nature and abilities. Although Maslow largely wrote with men in mind, Friedan argued that women, too, needed creative outlets aside from their duties as housewives and mothers.[5] Invoking her own experience as a suburban housewife with three children, Friedan claimed that a life of only domestic concerns was unsatisfying. Friedan's prescriptions were hardly revolutionary, even if another of her inspirations were the writings of Karl Marx. She believed that getting married and having children comprised a vital part of the full experience of womanhood, and she recognized that men and women had some essential differences.

In making her case, however, Friedan made numerous grandiose and absurd assertions. The stultifying existence of the suburban home (in her words, a "comfortable concentration camp") and the worship of the ultra-feminine homemaker, she claimed, made mothers so unhappy that they were directly responsible for rising homosexuality among young men. These neurotic super-moms allegedly produced Korean War soldiers who, once captured, proved especially spineless and inept.[6]

A Book You're Not Supposed to Read

10 Books that Screwed Up the World... and 5 Others that Didn't Help by Benjamin Wiker, Ph.D. (Washington, D.C.: Regnery, 2008). Wiker's excellent, even essential, book has a chapter devoted to Betty Friedan's *The Feminine Mystique*.

Friedan's work, put forward in her seminal 1963 book, *The Feminine Mystique*, relied heavily on her limited sampling of her college class-mates, supplemented by her own highly subjective interviews with a small cross-section of New York area women. She buttressed this with selective and somewhat misleading claims about the articles and advertising in women's magazines.[7]

Friedan was no scientist, and she was quite disingenuous about the supposed drudgery of her own life as a housewife. Her readers at the time were not informed that she had a full-time maid who washed her family's dishes and clothes. (Freidan later remarked that she never even learned how to operate a washer and dryer.[8]) She also downplayed the tremendous assistance she received from her husband, who gave up his own dreams of being a theater director in order to support his wife and children, then provided the money to hire press agents to fund his wife's literary ambitions.[9]

Friedan became the first president of the quintessential feminist organization, the National Organization for Women, a position from which she lobbied for the legalization of abortion. Unlike some other feminists, Friedan acknowledged the complexities of the issue, later writing that "such slogans as 'free abortion on demand' have connotations of sexual licentiousness...implying a certain lack of reverence for life and the mysteries of conception and birth which have been women's agony and ecstasy and defining value down through the ages....Being 'for abortion' is like being 'for mastectomy.'"[10]

If Friedan represented liberal feminism, Gloria Steinem was the radical. The offspring of a Jewish father and German-American mother, Steinem suffered after her once-affluent parents divorced. (Her mother suffered from mental illness and had to be repeatedly institutionalized.) The divorce forced Steinem into extreme poverty at age twelve, and compelled to her care for her own mother in a rat-infested house.[11]

Perhaps it was her difficult upbringing that made Steinem into an extremist. Although it is not true, as is commonly believed, that Steinem invented the phrase, "Women need men like a fish needs a bicycle," she did popularize it, and the missive expresses her general outlook on men. Throughout her life she repeatedly ended relationships when men appeared intent on marriage. When she did marry, it was at age sixty-five to an animal rights activist who died three years later. Steinem never had children; instead, her entire life was her career, punctuated by her founding of the feminist *Ms.* Magazine. But even in her business life, many of her aides and associates have often commented on the impossibility of really getting to know her.[12]

Rejecting so-called liberal feminism, Steinem describes herself as a radical feminist. Nearly the only aspect of her youth that she has discussed enthusiastically is an abortion she underwent in London in the 1950s. "If men could get pregnant," she maintains, "abortion would be a sacrament."[13] Like many radical feminists, Steinem has compared the role of a married woman to that of an underpaid whore.[14]

Inevitably, Friedan attacked Steinem and her allies as "female chauvinist boors" prone to male-bashing.[15] One especially emphatic difference between the Friedan and Steinem camps was their attitudes toward lesbianism. As president of the National Organization for Women, Friedan led not one but two purges of the group's lesbian radicals, warning that they posed a "lavender menace" to NOW and would alienate many women.

How to Lose Friends and Alienate People

"Her blatant hostility to and incomprehension of religion demonstrate why feminism, after its late-1960s resurgence, quickly lost three-quarters of its potential constituency among the great mass of ordinary women."

—Feminist **Camille Paglia**, on former National Organization for Women president Patricia Ireland, an adherent of NOW's radical lesbian wing[17]

...But Don't Question Their Patriotism

"Feminist leaders and some up-and-comers sat in a semicircle around [former NOW president Eleanor] Smeal, creating a devotional environment. Smeal...began a dissertation about the Straight-White-Religious-Right-Conservative-Republican-Male-Conspiracy against women, against feminists, and against anyone who wasn't like them.

"...America was a world of unrelenting racism, sexism, and homophobia, according to Smeal. It was the American system itself that was part of the problem. The 'tyranny of the majority' that democracy allowed had to be smashed and changed."

—former NOW Los Angeles chapter president **Tammy Bruce**, describing a feminist strategy session[20]

Friedan's warning was prescient. Since 1970, when Friedan was forced to relinquish its presidency, NOW has become increasingly dominated by lesbians and has lost much of its appeal to the mass of American women. Today NOW is virtually an appendage of the Democratic Party, and appears focused primarily on abortion and other wedge issues. As the head of NOW, in contrast, Friedan solicited support from Republicans and attended Republican national conventions.[16] She even invited William F. Buckley's likeminded sister, the Catholic conservative Patricia Buckley Bozell, to serve on NOW's board.

Shunting Friedan's followers aside, Steinem's radical clique gained control of NOW and came to preside over the whole feminist movement. In her path to power, Steinem allied herself with radical feminists whose theories ranged from the bizarre to the immoral. These included Andrea

Dworkin, who assailed the morality of *all* heterosexual sex; Ti-Grace Atkinson, a former NOW chapter president who attacks heterosexuality as a "reassuring reminder" of men's "class supremacy" and "a convenient reminder to the female of her class inferiority;"[18] and Kate Millet, a lesbian sufferer of bipolar disorder who insisted that sexual relationships between men and boys or between women and girls could be "wonderful."[19]

> ### A Book You're Not Supposed to Read
>
> *The Marriage Problem: How Our Culture Has Weakened Families* by James Q. Wilson (New York: Harper Collins, 2002).

Betty Friedan was far more representative of liberal women than was Gloria Steinem, but as is so often the case with liberal social movements, feminism was taken over by a radical minority that cleverly and ruthlessly pushed their opponents aside. Where Friedan paid respect to family conventions, the radicals often preached a nihilistic rejection of all conventional morality. Today, feminism exists as a collection of rote grievances promulgated by Women's Studies departments and groups like NOW.

The legacy of feminism

However marginalized it might seem, the feminist movement had a lasting impact on America: it was a key factor in the breakdown of the American family.

The feminists' most noteworthy achievement was the legalization of abortion. As previously mentioned, legalized abortion was a major goal of both liberal and radical feminists. The Supreme Court's ruling on *Roe v. Wade* in 1973, creating a right to abortion and striking down the abortion laws of all fifty states, was a huge victory for feminists. That victory came in a way that would become wearily familiar—from a politicized court rather than from democratic legislation.

The legalization of abortion had a dramatic impact on the American family, playing a key role in the rise in rates of premarital sex during the 1970s; people had more sex when abortion became legal, because even if birth control failed, the risk of sex leading to the unplanned birth of a child was lowered.[21] Marriage rates simultaneously fell, since it was now much easier for men to have sex without getting married—between 1970 and 2005, the marriage rate fell by a stunning 50 percent.[22] Ironically, the sixties feminists' predecessors warned against this exact scenario. As feminist historian Linda Gordon recounts, many nineteenth-century suffragettes and women's rights activists opposed abortion and birth control because they believed it would remove responsibility from men, encourage men to use and discard women, undermine marriage, and lead to widespread family breakdown.[23]

A second major contributing factor to family breakdown has been a change in divorce laws—another policy supported by radical feminists. Throughout the sixties, all fifty states had "at fault" divorce laws—if people wanted a divorce, they typically had to get their spouse's consent or else show that their spouse had committed some misdeed, such as infidelity. But beginning in 1969, with the vocal support of women's groups, states began introducing "no fault" divorce, allowing people to be granted a divorce absent any "fault" in their spouse's behavior. Unsurprisingly, when infidelity became less

Not What They Were Striving For

"The freedom that women were supposed to have found in the Sixties largely boiled down to easy contraception and abortion; things to make life easier for men, in fact."

— leftwing journalist **Julie Burchill**[24]

Stickin' It to the (Wo)Man

One the greatest beneficiaries of community property laws turned out to be former Students for a Democratic Society leader Tom Hayden, who married movie star and fellow leftwing activist Jane Fonda. Hayden cheated on Fonda, but thanks to community property laws, upon their divorce he was awarded roughly half the profits from Fonda's popular exercise videos—a cool $110 million.

penalized there was more of it, and when divorce was made easier divorce rates skyrocketed.[25]

What kind of no-fault divorce laws were best? Women's groups typically favored "community property," which generally means an even split of assets acquired during a marriage regardless of infidelity or other misdeeds by either party. These laws, approved in California, Texas, and other states, further reduced the penalties for infidelity and invited serial marriage.

Finally, feminists lobbied for more money to be given to women through Aid to Families with Dependent Children (AFDC), one of the federal government's chief welfare programs. Such appeals found a receptive audience in the administrations of Lyndon Johnson and even Richard Nixon; between 1965 and 1970, welfare benefits rose 69 percent. Since AFDC mostly funded unmarried women with children, however, the program's expansion simply increased the incentive for poor, unmarried women to have children while decreasing the incentive for them to get married or stay married. The feminist National Welfare Rights Organization, meanwhile, successfully worked to block congressional approval of Nixon administration proposals to require welfare recipients to work.[26] The result, as described in chapter 11, was further family breakdown and the onset of debilitating welfare dependence among many women, especially black women, that only subsided with the comprehensive welfare reform of 1996.

In short, it was much better to be a kid in a traditional family—which were most families—in the 1960s than it was to be a kid of parents who absorbed the anti-family ethos of the 1960s radicals who later dramatically remade the social mores of our country and made them so much more unfriendly to marriage, family, and fidelity.

Chapter Three

CIVIL RIGHTS AND UNCIVIL WRONGS: FROM FREEDOM RIDES TO "BURN, BABY, BURN"

More than anything else, it is the civil rights movement that has given us our view of the 1960s as a progressive decade in which, finally, all Americans, regardless of their skin color, secured equal rights to vote, to education, to compete for jobs, and to enjoy public accommodations. The original sixties civil rights activists fought bravely for these goals at a time when lynchings were still sometimes used to enforce racial segregation and submission. The Freedom Riders who traveled to Mississippi and Alabama to test desegregation laws in interstate busing knew they were risking their lives; most of their leaders were beaten or fired upon at one time or another. This violence was nothing new; it is well-known that Rosa Parks was arrested in 1955 in Montgomery, Alabama, for refusing to ride in the back of the bus, but it's less well-known that all the way back in 1942, Congress of Racial Equality (CORE) leader Bayard Rustin was thrashed by Nashville police for the same "crime."[1]

In 1947, during a precursor to the sixties Freedom Rides, Martin Walker (a crippled veteran) and Ray Sylvester were beaten by white mobs.[2] In Anniston, Alabama, in 1961, police allowed a mob of Klansmen to attack and firebomb a bus full of Freedom Riders, leaving dozens injured.[3] There were uncounted other acts of violence against peaceful civil rights protestors, including the murders of Martin Luther King Jr.,

Guess What?

- Black Americans' economic conditions improved more rapidly before the sixties civil rights movement than afterward

- The sixties urban riots were not caused by poverty and racism

- Cesar Chavez campaigned for the deportation of illegal immigrants

his ally Medgar Evers, and the three victims of the "Mississippi burning" killings, Andrew Goodman, James Chaney, and Michael Schwerner.

The movement's iconic leader, of course, was Southern Christian Leadership Conference (SCLC) president Martin Luther King Jr., a man who braved attack dogs, fire hoses, imprisonment, and truncheons. His speeches during the weeks leading up to his shooting in 1968 hinted that he anticipated his own death, yet King nonetheless continued advocating non-violent campaigns to achieve equality under the law.

Much of the civil rights movement is rightly remembered as heroic. Yet, like many aspects of the sixties, it has become shrouded in mythology and subject to politically correct revisions.

The biggest myth surrounding the civil rights movement is the conventional wisdom that there was virtually no progress in the economic, educational, and social condition of black Americans until the Civil Rights Act of 1964 was approved. Contrary to popular belief, these conditions steadily improved from the 1920s onward. Consider these facts:

- The percentage of black families under the poverty level fell from 87 percent in 1940 to just 47 percent in 1960.[4]
- Adjusted for inflation, the average income of skilled black workers doubled relative to whites between 1936 and 1959.[5]
- The education gap between black and white adults fell from three years in 1940 to two years in 1960, even as education levels rose rapidly in both groups.[6]
- The number of blacks with technical and professional occupations doubled between 1954 and 1964, and the absolute number of jobs gained by blacks grew more from 1961 to 1962 than from 1964 to 1966.[7] In contrast, the percentage of gainfully employed blacks working in managerial positions did *not* increase from 1964 to 1967—the three years following passage of the Civil Rights Act.[8]

- Between 1940 and 1950 the proportion of all American college students attending historically black colleges rose by 350 percent.[9] At the same time, by the early 1960s more and more blacks were attending integrated colleges—so much so that more were attending integrated colleges by 1963 than were enrolled in historically black colleges, notwithstanding the tremendous growth in black schools.

- Segregation received major blows in the late 1940s and early 1950s when vital sectors of American society such as the military were integrated. Discrimination in employment for the federal government was banned by executive order in 1942. Jackie Robinson broke baseball's color barrier in 1947, around the same time that barriers crumbled to the hiring of blacks in professional football.

In sharp contrast, the mid-to-late 1960s was a disastrous time for the youngest and poorest blacks. The Great Society programs, enjoying deep support among civil rights activists, were a calamity, ushering in a decades-long process of breakdown in the black family, as discussed in chapter 11. The civil rights movement might have succeeded in gaining political equality for blacks, but its victories could not mask the concurrent tragedy of the economic and social collapse of the black family, a disaster that has done more to harm black America than any other single factor over the last four decades.

In addition, as with feminism, the civil rights movement, after its early successes, became propelled by radicals rather than by moderate liberals, so that its just goals of eliminating racial discrimination quickly devolved into the primary goal of enforcing reverse discrimination; instead of a color-blind society, it began advocating racial quotas; and, at its worst, instead of following the path of non-violence, it promoted racial hatred.

From anti-discrimination to "positive discrimination"

Perhaps the biggest failing of the civil rights movement was that it worked toward spreading affirmative action programs as a leading goal. The most common justification for this kind of reverse discrimination—giving race-based preferences to blacks over whites in employment, college admissions, and the dispensation of government contracts—was that it was needed to "level the playing field." But in many industries outside the South, blacks were not performing substantially differently than whites before the advent of federally mandated affirmative action programs in 1969, when one adjusts for differences in age and education. A 1969–70 study of blacks with doctorates, for instance, found that they were on average paid better than whites with comparable degrees.[10]

The embrace of affirmative action by civil rights activists entailed a crucial decision to pursue not just equal opportunity, but equal outcomes. It was no longer enough that blacks have equal access to jobs and university admissions—now the government was asked to guarantee that a set number of blacks actually were hired or admitted, regardless of ability. This was part of a long-term trend by civil rights activists to define their ever-growing list of demands as "civil rights issues." Martin Luther King Jr., for example, ultimately declared the Vietnam War to be a civil rights issue.

King, in fact, showed one of his greatest failings when he decided to support affirmative action, a policy that directly contradicted his famous dream that his children would be judged "not by the color of their

I Have a Dream—of Race Preferences

The insistence on equal outcomes was already evident in the name of one of the most renowned events of the civil rights movement—the 1963 March on Washington for Jobs and Freedom, site of Martin Luther King Jr.'s "I Have a Dream" speech. Note that marchers were not demanding equal *consideration* for jobs, but the provision of actual jobs.

skin, but by the content of their character." He discussed the issue in an interview with, of all things, *Playboy* magazine, which asked if he thought it was "fair to request a multi-billion dollar program of preferential treatment for the Negro, or any other minority group." King responded,

> I do indeed. Can any fair-minded citizen deny that the Negro has been deprived? Few people reflect that for two centuries the Negro was enslaved, and robbed of any wages [or] potential accrued wealth which could have been the legacy of his descendants. All of America's wealth today could not adequately compensate its Negroes for his centuries of exploitation and discrimination. It is an economic fact that a program such as I propose would certainly cost far less than any computation of two centuries of unpaid wages plus accumulated interest. In any case, I do not intend that this program of economic aid should apply only to the Negro; it should benefit the disadvantaged of *all* races. [emphasis in original][11]

However brilliant this may be rhetorically, the logic is baffling. Why should Korean immigrants, Mexican illegal aliens, Irish Catholics, or any other group benefit from a program designed to help the descendants of slaves? And what about more recent black immigrants, from Africa or the Caribbean, who have no familial experience of slavery in this country? What of mixed-raced blacks with mostly white ancestry? Or more fundamentally, what about a color-blind society that accepts that everyone's starting point is inevitably different, but that no special hurdles should be put in the way of letting all excel through hard work—as innumerable ethnic, racial, and religious groups have done in this country throughout its history?

The racial spoils game that began in the 1960s has now come to involve city, state, and federal contracting, the licensing of TV stations

Dissent Is Patriotic

While the vast majority of civil rights activists came to demand equal outcomes through affirmative action programs, there were some dissenters,
such as Bayard Rustin, who helped found the Congress of Racial Equality and
the Southern Christian Leadership Conference and had risked his life to
oppose Jim Crow long before Rosa Parks and Martin Luther King Jr. first
attracted public notice. Rustin pointed out in *Commentary* magazine in 1965
that some of his peers were "now concerned not merely with removing the
barriers to full *opportunity* but with achieving the fact of *equality*" [empha-
sis in original]. For the civil rights movement, he warned, this was "an evolu-
tion calling its very name into question."[12]

and cable networks, and admission to colleges and professional schools.
Large corporations know they must hire a certain number of minority
employees—regardless of ability—or face investigation by state and federal equal opportunity commissions. By 1995 affirmative action programs
covered 95,000 companies with 27 million employees.[13] Universities now
routinely judge applicants with different standards for whites, Hispanics,
blacks and Asians. This, sadly, is the true legacy of the civil rights movement—a sad epitaph for a cause that once sought to achieve a color-blind
society.

Ironically, civil rights activists insisted that the Civil Rights Act of
1964 would *prohibit* reverse discrimination. Title VII of the Act specified
that "[n]othing contained in this Title shall be interpreted to require any
employer...to grant preferential treatment to any individual or to any
group because of the race, color, religion, sex or national origin of such
individual or group." During debate over the bill in the Senate, Hubert

Humphrey promised that the Act would not "require an employer to achieve any sort of racial balance in his work force by giving preferential treatment to any individual or group."[14] In fact, he promised to eat the pages of the bill if any such language could be found. Many Senate Republicans, led by Everett Dirksen of Illinois, agreed to support the bill on the condition that amendments were added to prohibit the use of racial quotas and race-based preferences.

But once the bill was approved, courts interpreted it in the exact opposite way, with the vociferous support of civil rights activists. This shift happened with astonishing speed—within little more than a decade of the Act's approval, federal contracts were being given to minority contractors who were not the lowest bidders.[15]

This had a particularly dramatic effect on universities. Harvard professor Nathan Glazer notes that within three years of the beginning of federal affirmative action "mandates," San Francisco State College—with the approval of the federal government—announced a plan for race-based hiring according to the city's demographics; Cornell's president openly called for hiring "unqualified or marginally qualified" minorities; and the U.S. Health, Education, and Welfare Department demanded that the Religious Studies department at an Ivy League school eliminate requirements that its instructors know Greek and Hebrew, the languages in which the Bible was written, because not enough minorities knew them.[16]

Warning: Affirmative Action May Be Damaging to Your Economy

The spread of affirmative action found a natural expression in the Community Reinvestment Act of 1977, which effectively forced banks to make loans to unqualified minorities. Adopted as a means to combat alleged discrimination in bank lending practices, the law played a central role in devastating many banks and sparking the present subprime mortgage crisis.

Not only does affirmative action seem inherently unfair and foster resentment (both among beneficiaries, who know their promotion is exclusively race-based, and those who lose jobs or academic placements because of government-sanctioned discrimination), it has failed in its purported goal of improving the economic condition of blacks. Consider, the annual number of blacks scoring at the highest level on law school admissions tests was more than twice as high in the 1960s as it was in the 1980s;[17] the difference in black and white scores on graduate school entrance exams are even larger than their difference on undergraduate entrance exams;[18] and minority students admitted under preferential programs have far lower graduation rates, especially at public universities.[19] Thus, far from helping to "level the playing field," affirmative action has acted as a powerful disincentive to black achievement, and certainly

The Pro-Civil Rights Party?

Although the Democratic Party has claimed the mantra of the civil rights movement, it was southern Democrats who led an historic filibuster against the Civil Rights Act of 1964. Most dogged in opposing the bill was West Virginia senator, former Ku Klux Klan member, and future Democratic majority leader Robert Byrd. Byrd's fourteen-hour filibuster against the bill was the longest in Senate history. His speech included references to the supposed segregationist ideas of saints Luke and Paul.

In total, the filibuster led by the "yellow dog" Democrats ran for ten million words over 534 hours, filling up 63,000 pages of the Congressional Record.[20] Ultimately, 62 percent of Democratic congressmen and 60 percent of Democratic senators voted for the bill, compared to 80 percent of Republican congressmen and 82 percent of Republican senators.[21]

done nothing to restore the calamitous dissolution of stable black families that would have been, and were, the true source of black academic and economic advancement.

Jumping on the bandwagon

In the mid-to-late 1960s, a steady stream of hucksters, crooks, rabble-rousers, and self-declared radicals proclaimed themselves to be civil rights leaders, seeking to profit from the ever-expanding "civil rights" industry. These charlatans replaced the Freedom Riders and Christian ministers who led the early, heroic campaign against segregation. Eventually, the civil rights groups themselves were transformed from altruistic, integrationist organizations into corrupt, separatist ones.

One of the first of the new civil rights "leaders" to emerge in the late 1960s was the West Indian immigrant Stokely Carmichael. During a June 1966 march of an old-line civil rights organization, the Student Non-Violent Coordinating Committee (SNCC), Carmichael voiced a demand for "Black Power." Recognizing this as a call for black separatism, King and Roy Wilkins, former head of the NAACP, criticized Carmichael's declaration. But Carmichael's radical allies later managed to take over the NAACP, provoking Wilkins to leave the group.

Likewise, the Congress of Racial Equality (CORE) fell into the hands of men like Alfred Black, who once declared that "a black man today is either a radical or an Uncle Tom," clearly suggesting that King and Wilkins belonged in the latter category. CORE director Floyd McKissick, a black power advocate, even hinted at violent reprisals against civil rights moderates, speaking of the need for "dealing with those Negroes who sell us out—who betray their people."[22]

King's murder on April 4, 1968, set the stage for a particularly unscrupulous opportunist to stake a claim to leadership of the civil rights movement. Jesse Jackson, who was at the Memphis motel when King was assassinated, appeared in interviews and public appearances the day after King's killing. Declaring that his sweater was stained with King's blood, he asserted that King had died in his arms and that he was the last person to whom King had spoken. But Jackson's claims to be steeped in the blood of his martyred patron were disputed by others present at the scene, who denied that Jackson even came close to King after his shooting. "My guess is that Jesse smeared the blood on his shirt after getting it off the balcony," remarked musician Ben Branch, who was with Jackson during the shooting.[23] It was a fitting launching pad for a man who would make a lucrative career out of exploiting the memory of the sixties civil rights movement. Where King risked his life to end segregation, the only thing Jackson risks is ruffling his tailored suits as he shakes down corporations for donations for his cronies.

Keep Hoax Alive

"I am sure Reverend Jackson would not say to *me* that he cradled Dr. King. I am sure that Reverend Jackson would realize that I was the person who was on the balcony with Dr. King and did not leave his side until he was pronounced dead at St. Joseph's Hospital in Memphis. I am sure that he would not say to *me* that he even came near Dr. King after Doc was shot."

— the **Reverend Ralph D. Abernathy**, King's chosen successor as leader of the Southern Christian Leadership Conference[24]

Who was Malcolm X?

The mass media is sympathetic to all of the self-proclaimed civil rights leaders of the 1960s, but it is particularly hard to explain its worshipful tone toward the erstwhile Malcolm Little, the man most of us know as Malcolm X. This adulatory view has trickled down to popular culture: from the T-shirts emblazoned with Malcolm X's face to Hollywood's glamorized biopics, America has chosen a very unlikely candidate to memorialize as a civil rights hero.

A part-white native of East Lansing, Michigan, Malcolm X gained fame as a leader of the Black Muslim sect, which he joined in the 1940s while serving time for robbery in a Massachusetts prison. Much of the conventional wisdom about Malcolm X derives from his autobiography, written with the assistance of *Roots* author Alex Haley, or from Spike Lee's motion picture based on the book. Both detail his life as a criminal, his years in prison, his conversion to the Nation of Islam sect, and his rise to prominence as a promoter of its heretical version of Islam. In the book, he tells stories about his close ties with notorious gangsters like "Dutch" Schultz. In the movie, we see him dressed in fancy suits, working at the top of the Harlem criminal underworld. The film's not–so–subtle message is seductive: that you can get great clothes and beautiful women through a life of crime—and then leave that life and do even better.

Much worse, however, than the celebration of Malcolm X's criminality and the bizarre mantling of him as a hero of the civil rights movement, is the blithe popular acceptance, promoted by the liberal media, that he was somehow a wise and admirable man. Malcolm X's philosophy of hate and racial supremacy was in fact not so different from that of the Ku Klux Klan, only weirder. The Nation of Islam teaches that blacks were the only people on earth until six thousand years ago, when a certain Doctor Yaqub created whites in a laboratory experiment. Whites, the sect believes, are literally devils incapable of kindness, decency, or love.

Not as Advertised

Malcolm X was something of a con artist—especially after he left prison. For example, he frequently claimed that his father had been killed by white supremacists when in fact his father was run over by a streetcar.[25] What's more, while he portrayed himself as having been a major criminal kingpin at one point, biographers suggest he was merely a small-time hoodlum who barely got by with the aid of extra money earned as a gay hustler.[26]

It is often supposed that by the end of his life Malcolm X had softened his racial attitudes. After all, some say, Malcolm X left the Nation of Islam a year before his death, and he said in his autobiography that he no longer believed all whites were devils. This is strongly suggested in Spike Lee's hagiographic movie, in the scene where Malcolm X sees people of many races arriving in Mecca. Yet, although he might have renounced some of the Nation of Islam's nuttier beliefs, Malcolm X was to the end of his life an anti-white advocate of racial separatism. As he himself explained, he didn't leave the Nation of Islam because of its hateful ideology, but because he was offended by the sexual affairs of the sect's leader, Elijah Muhammad.[27]

Those who see Malcolm X as a "civil rights" leader point out that he went to the Senate to support the Civil Rights Act, but they tend to ignore the scorn he heaped upon moderate civil rights campaigns, such as his dismissive reference to the 1963 March on Washington as "the farce on Washington."[28] It was, he said, an event "run by whites in front of a statue of a president who has been dead for a hundred years and who didn't like us when he was alive."

The circumstances of Malcolm X's death in 1965 have been obscured and rewritten in order to project an image of martyrdom. In the Spike Lee film, his killer's identity is left ambiguous. There is little doubt, however, that Malcolm X was shot and killed by members of the Nation of Islam on the orders of its leader and founder, Elijah Muhammad. Two months before Malcolm X's murder, Muhammad had told his aide, Louis Farrakhan, that Malcolm X's head "should be cut off"; Nation of Islam periodicals had called for his killing; and Farrakhan flunkies were caught at the scene and convicted of the crime. The obvi-

---

☮ ☮ ☮ ☮ ☮ ☮ ☮ ☮ ☮

A Real Sympathetic Man

"Being an old farmboy myself, chickens coming home to roost never did make me sad; they've always made me glad."

— **Malcolm X**, commenting on the assassination of President Kennedy

---

ous motive for the killing was that Malcolm X had been trying to take away adherents—and major sources of money—from the Nation of Islam by seizing control of a mosque that functioned as the sect's Harlem head-quarters.

Who was Malcolm X? He was at the forefront of a string of sixties black leaders who, in marked contrast to King, purposefully straddled the line between political activism and criminality.

Who were the Black Panthers?

Once the most notorious and violent of the sixties black power groups—but one loved by 1960s liberals besotted with radical chic—was the Black Panther party, whose members made their name by shooting policemen and made their money by selling drugs and running other criminal rackets like prostitution rings and extortion schemes against bar and liquor store owners.

Known formally as the Black Panther Party for Self-Defense, the Panthers were founded under the leadership of Huey Newton and Bobby Seale in Oakland, California, in 1966. According to the testimony of an admiring disciple and childhood friend in his authorized biography, Newton supported himself during the early 1960s through burglary, petty theft, and confidence games.[29] Sometimes engaging in armed robbery, he also stole from the cars of people rushing into hospital emergency rooms.[30]

Newton's friendship and affection for his fellow self-professed political activist, Bobby Seale, began at their first meeting when Seale told Newton that he owned four guns. Commenting on Newton's recent

Devouring Their Own

David Horowitz, who once worked with the Black Panthers, cites the Panthers' murder of his friend, Panther bookkeeper Betty Van Patter, as a key event in his transformation into a conservative.

scrape with a homeless man, Seale proclaimed that he would have pumped lead into the bum's stomach. Soon after that conversation, Newton was imprisoned for stabbing a man in the back with a steak knife during a house party.[31]

Admirers of Malcolm X, the two men decided to set up their own "party." When the semi-literate pair produced the party's brief manifesto, they had to first run it by Seale's brother Artie, a Berkeley graduate student, to fix the grammar.[32]

Heavily influenced by the ideas of Karl Marx and the radical psychiatrist Frantz Fanon, the party's platform was a mixture of Communist rabble-rousing and racial separatism. It asserted that "the federal government is responsible and obligated to give every man employment or a guaranteed income. We believe that if the white American businessmen will not give full employment, the means of production should be taken from the businessmen and placed in the community." Later paragraphs called for reparations for slavery, blacks-only jury trials for black defendants, complete exemption of blacks from military service, release of all blacks from jail, and a U.N.-sponsored plebiscite for self-determination in the "black colony" (ghetto neighborhoods). The manifesto ended with a parody of the Declaration of Independence that called for black revolution.[33]

The group attracted numerous ex-cons, including Eldridge Cleaver, a convicted rapist who hailed the rape of white women by black men as an "insurrectionary act," and George Jackson, who had served a decade in jail by age 28. Consequently, criminality suffused the organization, extending even to murder. Panthers tortured to death New Haven Black Panther member Alex Rackley, who had been falsely accused of being a government agent; Jackson took a Student Non-Violent Coordinating Committee member hostage and forced him to play Russian Roulette; and Jackson's men shot a radical lawyer named Fay Stender, who had once worked on their behalf. The group's misogyny also spilled into the realm of criminality—when confronted with the accusation that he had raped a fourteen-year-old girl, Cleaver responded that he wished she were twelve.[34]

The Panthers dressed in militant outfits with black berets, threatened the police, and engaged in a lot of political theater that enthralled the press. One of Newton's more creative ideas was to show up with a group of visibly armed Panthers at the state capitol building in Sacramento. The group's trajectory took a sinister turn on October 28, 1967, when Newton shot two police officers, one fatally, following a routine traffic stop. Newton pleaded self-defense, a tough case to make given that he had shot Officer John Frey repeatedly in the back. Although a jury found him guilty, the conviction was overturned two years later on a technicality.

That Doesn't Sound Very Progressive

"The only correct position for women in the movement is prone."

— Black Panther leader **Jewel Cook**[35]

The case drew even greater publicity for the Panthers, whose membership rapidly increased. Becoming particularly popular among local street gangs, the party eventually attracted up to 7,000 members, according to some reports.[36]

The Panthers compiled a horrific record of carnage to rival that of the most hardened mafia families. In 1969 alone there were 348 arrests of Panthers for rape, armed robbery, burglary, and murder.[37] By the end of that year, no fewer than twenty-eight Panthers had been killed in internecine rivalries or in gun battles with the police. Even the liberal *New Yorker* magazine acknowledged that all the shoot-outs were instigated by the Panthers.[38] As for the party's internal feuding, it stemmed from a clash between factions led by Cleaver and Newton, respectively, over Cleaver's ambition to spark an immediate race war.

The group's descent into raw criminality reflected the moral character of its leaders. Having become addicted to cocaine, in 1974 Newton was widely believed to have butchered a seventeen-year-old prostitute named

The Panthers' Greatest Hits

The long list of crimes committed by the Black Panthers includes:

- stealing weapons from the Camp Pendleton marine base and plotting an attack on San Quentin Prison to release its black inmates
- shooting and killing a judge in a Marin County courtroom
- taking over gambling and drug rackets at the Soledad and Folsom prisons
- organizing a hostage-taking incident at San Quentin prison in which Panthers slit the throats of three guards and two white inmates
- scheming to poison the Chicago water supply[39]

Kathleen Smith for allegedly insulting him. Facing murder charges, he fled to Cuba. While there, in 1977 Newton met and befriended Jim Jones, who a year later engineered the mass suicide of nearly one thousand of his cult followers in the Jonestown compound in Guyana. Returning to America in 1977 and beating the rap for Smith's murder, Newton was convicted in 1989 of embezzling funds from a Panther-organized school.

There is much speculation that Newton deliberately provoked his own murder. On August 22, 1989, Newton organized an impromptu crack-smoking party at which he confessed to a local homeless man and fellow crack addict his guilt in the murder of Officer Frey. Then Newton went to see an Oakland drug dealer named Tyrone Robinson whom Newton had robbed twice before.[40] Newton perhaps anticipated that he would not survive a third attempt to rob Robinson, who indeed shot and killed him.

Perhaps the most remarkable aspect of the Black Panthers is how this violent gang of thieves, drug addicts, and racial separatists became a *cause célèbre* among radical intellectuals and celebrities, earning the support of Marlon Brando, Yale president Kingman Brewster, French playwright Jean Genet, and conductor Leonard Bernstein, among many others.[42] For most of these people, the Panthers provided a chance for what the French call *nostalgia de la boue*, the thrill and glamour gained from occasionally associating with sociopaths. This also seems to be the motivation of several female defense attorneys who represented Panther members and had affairs with them.

For many young leftists, however, fantasizing about the Panthers was not an amusement or a passing fancy but a self-deluding obsession. A mania for the Panthers gripped many elite universities; by 1969 it was not unusual for dorm rooms at Harvard or Columbia to be adorned with posters of Newton scornfully staring ahead with a rifle clasped in each hand, wearing his black beret and seated on a rattan throne. Panther leaders were adored much as Hollywood heartthrobs are today. The Black Panthers were, in the words of Students for a Democratic Society leader Tom Hayden, "America's Vietcong," the guerrillas who would lead the revolution.

Not a Great Role Model

"Mr. Cleaver drifted in his enthusiasms. He opened a boutique for the trousers he created featuring what he called the Cleaver sleeve. He embraced various religions. He ran a recycling business for a while, but other recyclers accused him of stealing their garbage. He was treated for addiction to crack cocaine in 1990. A crack charge two years later was dropped because of an illegal search, but in 1994 Berkeley police found him staggering about with a severe, never fully explained, head injury and a rock of crack in his pocket."

— from the *New York Times* obituary of **Eldridge Cleaver**[41]

What caused the 1960s urban riots?

On August 11, 1965, something major came out of something minor.

The trivial matter was a black drunk driver getting arrested after failing a sobriety test in the Watts section of Los Angeles. After a policeman handcuffed the driver, however, an angry crowd began threatening the cop and throwing stones and bottles at the back-up officers who arrived. A local disc jockey on a black radio station whipped up the community with cries of "Burn, baby, burn." Before long, mobs of young men were rampaging, looting stores, and setting fires.

Initially, the rioters, bolstered by large numbers of local street gang members, busied themselves with stoning and beating whites. One black witness remarked, "It's a wonder that anyone with white skin got out of there alive....Every time a car with whites in it entered the area the word spread like lightning down the street: 'Here comes Whitey—get him!'"[43] A white reporter and photographer for the *LA Times* barely escaped, for example, even though they never left their car.[44]

By early the following morning, the thrust of the rioting had switched from bashing whites to theft. The pillaging began at a supermarket on Avalon and 188th Street, and soon every store in the neighborhood was a target for looters. Rioters shot at police helicopters, and commercial planes were re-routed away from the neighborhood after bullets were fired at them as well.[45]

During six days of rioting, thirty-four people were killed, more than a thousand were injured, and 977 buildings were damaged. Most of the victims were local black residents not serving in any official capacity.[46] But thirty-six firemen, more than ninety police officers, and numerous National Guard troops and government officials were also injured. Most of the stores that were destroyed were black-owned, with total property damage exceeding $200 million.

The riots were not quickly suppressed, largely because there was no direction from higher up. California governor Pat Brown was vacationing in Greece, and President Johnson initially refused to take action or even

Money Well Spent?

Stanford University spent $1 million on Huey Newton's private papers.

to acknowledge the gravity of the problem. According to Johnson's domestic policy advisor, Joseph Califano, "He refused to look at the cables from Los Angeles.... He refused to take calls from the generals who were requesting government planes to fly in the National Guard.... We needed decisions from him. But he simply wouldn't respond."[47] This was dereliction on a massive scale. Meanwhile, in the absence of direction from city, state, or federal authorities, the local police precinct captain in charge decided not to give his subordinates orders to fire on looters. Stopping the riots eventually required a force of almost 15,000 National Guardsmen—a whole army division.

The Watts riots became the model for other urban riots over the next three years, always in cities where the rioters thought they could get away with it because of weak political leadership. The riots of the 1960s weren't caused by racism and poverty, as liberals maintained. Urban riots didn't erupt, for instance, in Southern cities with large numbers of poor blacks, like Atlanta and Dallas. They erupted in cities like Newark and Detroit in 1967, killing twenty-three people and forty-three people, respectively. In both cities there was a woeful lack of local authority and a total absence of willpower to restore law and order.

The Real Root Cause of the Riots

According to sociologist Edward Banfield, the rioting in Watts was "mainly for fun and profit."[48]

In 1968, following Martin Luther King's assassination, riots broke out in a hundred more cities, leading to forty-six deaths and 3,000 injuries. The worst rioting that year was in the city that had the most predominant black middle-class, with the best job opportunities for minorities: Washington, D.C. The capital's rioters followed the lead of black power proponent Stokely Carmichael who, with a gun in his waistband, led an enraged mob through the city, demanding that shop owners close as a show of respect for King—or else. Carmichael had an additional bit of advice for the mob: "Go home and get your guns." In the resulting chaos, 700 fires were started throughout the city.[49] Although plenty of black businesses went up in flames, rioters especially sought out white-owned stores, provoking black owners to put signs up indicating their racial identity.

To attribute the riots to black anger over substandard housing or the lack of job opportunities is simplistic at best and more than a little naïve. In fact, studies of black youths in Los Angeles after the Watts riot showed they were not disaffected but actually highly optimistic about the future.[50] Polls of those arrested revealed that looters were more angered by the prices in local stores than by police brutality.[51] Propelled by the overall zeitgeist of black power, the riots were an expression of a new-found sense of power and entitlement, a gathering consciousness that something was *owed* to blacks and that whites were now afraid. Most of all, the riots were practical demonstrations that mobs could take the law into their own hands when a violent, active will was only confronted by liberal guilt and spinelessness.

Cesar Chavez: Labor organizer and best buddy of the INS

Cesar Chavez (born Cesario Chavez, 1927–1993) was arguably the most morally upstanding of the sixties civil rights leaders. Chavez wasn't motivated by money, like Jesse Jackson, and he wasn't a philanderer like Martin Luther King Jr. A devout Catholic and father of eight, he often began meetings with prayers and led pickets while holding Catholic icons. If he sought publicity, he was sincere in wishing to use it for his cause. Chavez's main goal was simply to improve the lives of California field hands.

However, what most people do not know about Chavez, the most successful and famous farm-worker in American history, is that while he urged boycotts of California grapes or lettuce to protest the conditions endured by farm-workers, he was equally devoted to helping government agencies deport illegal aliens.

Chavez viewed illegals as competitors for jobs with the native-born members of his union, the National Farm Workers Association. It was not strikes and boycotts but Chavez's campaign against illegal immigrants that was his most effective tool to force growers to negotiate with his union. When employers' illegal workers were rounded up and deported, the bosses had to sit down with Chavez and talk about higher pay. Chavez himself admitted that his first major strike, which came against a landowner named Robert DiGiorgio, succeeded because he "called some friends I had in the State Division of Labor Law Enforcement. In about two days we were able to get all of the *braceros* [Mexican immigrant workers] pulled out, about three hundred of them, and the [striking] women got their jobs back."[52]

Reporting on illegal immigrants and filing complaints against them became one of the union's major activities. In fact, when President Johnson's attorney general, Ramsey Clark, came to California during a 1967 strike, Chavez led a huge protest criticizing Clark for not deporting enough illegals.[53]

This was not the only aspect of Chavez's leadership that might give many liberals qualms today. Chavez established his union virtually as an autocracy—and naturally made himself the autocrat. As even a worshipful biographer was forced to concede,

> The farmworkers union had ranch committees—committees
> elected by members on the ranches—but those committees did
> not have the autonomy, authority or legal protections usually

enjoyed by a local union. Chavez could dismiss the ranch committee leaders whenever they did not please him. Thus Chavez created a union structure that gave himself and the executive board total control.[54]

Still, compared to some of the other icons of the 1960s civil rights movement tainted by ties to Communists, criminality, corruption, hate groups, and the creation of a racial spoils system, Chavez's autocratic union doesn't seem so bad.

The civil rights gains of the 1960s were great steps forward, but as with so much of that decade, progress in one direction—in terms of achieving equal rights—was often paid for by a radicalism that was terribly destructive and left a good cause hijacked to bad ends.

Chapter Four

☮

THE INTELLECTUALS: DID THEY HAVE IT ALL FIGURED OUT?

George Orwell once remarked that some ideas are so wrong that only a very intelligent person could believe in them. When it comes to the intellectuals of the 1960s, Orwell's quip is right on the mark. Professors, writers, and other elite thinkers of the decade were carried away with bizarre, extremist social theories that could not even get a serious hearing among the general public, imbued as it was with common sense. The sixties intellectual class inexplicably became enraptured with these ideas, showing a nihilistic determination to tear down American society and all its institutions, customs, and values. Certain elite circles amused themselves by discussing these theories as if they had some kind of merit, then discarded them as the disposable philosophies they really were while taking no responsibility for the harm—often grievous—they had inflicted.

The treason of the clerks, part I: It's a mad, mad world

As cities became marred by rioting during the 1960s, with crime rates doubling in the decade, middle-class residents fled to the suburbs. The urban centers they left behind were becoming not only dangerous, but squalid. Graffiti began to cover the sides of subways and storefronts. Thieves broke into abandoned buildings, stripping them of their copper pipes and leaving the buildings useless wrecks. Police and fire truck sirens were heard at all hours. Parks were left to decay, and the sides of roadways became cluttered with litter. By the end of the decade, legal go-go bars—strip clubs—were opening up next to respectable hotels.

This urban decay was cause for alarm and dismay by just about every sector of society except one: the intellectuals. What mainstream America recognized as disgraceful urban blight, many intellectuals celebrated as a kind of twisted form of transgressive art.

Standing at the forefront of the pro-blight clique was perhaps the most pivotal writer of the decade, Norman Mailer. Mailer had great facility with words, much ambition, and a snide yet engaging sense of humor. But beyond these qualities, it is hard to conceive how anyone could have made a worse novelist. After all, Mailer was singularly lacking in psychological depth or insight, he was self-absorbed, and his mind functioned largely at the level of adolescent fantasy. That such a figure proclaimed that his novels would surpass the works of Leo Tolstoy is comical. But Mailer's drive, his knack for self-promotion, and his ability to conjure precisely the trendy notions that would fascinate intellectual circles at a given moment made him far more famous than Isaac Bashevis Singer, Saul Bellow, Richard Yates, and many other superior writers of the time.

In his 1957 essay "The White Negro," Mailer promoted a new hero of American society—the psychopathic criminal. Since the criminal is not guided by the rigid rules of conformist society, Mailer proposed, it is he whom creative people should seek to emulate. Scrawling graffiti was good. So, too, was the hoodlum who "beat in the brains of a candy-store keeper." This was an act of daring and independence, an existential deed. Mailer's choice of a candy-store owner as a deserving victim was revealing. The Jewish Mailer was celebrating the murder of a small merchant in a then stereotypically Jewish field. In this way, as do many extremists on both the Left and the Right, he equated Jews with the role of the entrepreneur and the despised bourgeoisie. The values of the nebbishy but civilized white businessman were depicted as contemptible—as were, by extension, those of middle-class blacks or any other law-abiding group. Admirable instead was the predatory black man with a long rap sheet and an indifference to the wants and needs of others. Here was the embryonic ethos behind the destructive hedonism of the 1970s and of a later generation's gangster rap music.

Mailer articulated these ideas further through his fictional works, including his 1965 novel *An American Dream*. Written in the aftermath of Mailer's own stabbing of his second wife, the book celebrates its hero, Stephen Rojack, a sleazy late-night talk show host who gets away with killing his wife by throwing her out an upper-floor window. Immediately after killing her, Rojack sodomizes his maid, to her great delight. He then runs off with a sexy blonde singer to Las Vegas, where he uses his psychic powers to win at roulette and live a life of hedonism. Extraordinarily enough, the book was widely praised, especially by critics like the *New York Times*'s Eliot Fremont-Smith, who wanted to show that they were "hip" to the new values being promoted by society's ostensibly daring thinkers.

The idea that middle-class "squares" were the real problem was also expressed in Ken Kesey's acclaimed novel, *One Flew Over the Cuckoo's Nest*. Over the years, conservatives like Tom Wolfe have shown affection for Kesey because he was a libertarian and, as was demonstrated by his following novel, *Sometimes a Great Notion*, he was skeptical of unions. But the values advocated in *One Flew Over the Cuckoo's Nest* are similar to those of Mailer's *An American Dream*. In Kesey's (considerably better) story, published in 1962, a criminal named Randle McMurphy is brought to a mental hospital after feigning insanity

Unlucky with Women

Norman Mailer took some criticism for being married six times and having numerous mistresses. In his favor, however, of all these women, he only stabbed one of them.

as a means to avoid the county jail. Offended by his easy sexual manner, the domineering ward nurse has him subjected to electroshock therapy and then lobotomized. The message: those running our institutions are the true crazies, while he who avidly pursues his own urges outside of society's bounds is noble if misunderstood. The pursuit of personal liberation is deemed an absolute good.

The idea that sanity and insanity are relative and subjective concepts was a popular notion among sixties intellectuals. This assertion won adherents through the writings of another seminal figure, the Scottish psychiatrist R. D. Laing. Laing had won a youthful following early in the decade for his books, among them *The Divided Self: An Existential Study in Self and Madness*, which was first published in 1960. Like Gloria Steinem, Laing was in the business of selling a philosophy of life that even the most casual observer had to suspect was a response to extreme problems in his own family and his own life. Both of Laing's parents were mentally disordered, and by his own reckoning he suffered from alcoholism and depression.

Trained as a medical doctor and psychoanalyst, Laing had been taught that the roots of schizophrenia lay principally in biological causes and not life experiences. This was the belief of Freud, and it was powerfully supported by the development during the 1950s of the first antipsychotic medications, drugs like Thorazine and Haldol. These medicines can end or deter psychotic episodes in patients suffering from schizophrenia—strong proof of the organic origins of the disease, evidence that was further demonstrated in succeeding decades.

Laing, however, had different ideas. At a time when the most basic concepts of truth and reality were under attack, Laing found a ready audience for his view that the insane were merely people scarred by their own experiences, who were in further conflict with a confused society. In fact, an inability to comprehend reality might actually be a unique insight.

Therefore, Laing insisted, the children of troubled parents—people like Laing himself—needed empathy rather than drug treatment. Laing's philosophy was about as sound as his character: during the course of his career arguing that mental hospitals might be unnecessary, he fathered ten children by four women, keeping up few extended contacts with either the mothers or his offspring.

Nearly as widely read as Laing was Harvard psychology professor B. F. Skinner, who assaulted the idea of personal individuality and autonomy. Influenced by the research of Soviet scientist Ivan Pavlov, Skinner created his famous Skinner boxes to hold and manipulate rats, which could request food by pressing a lever with their feet. Skinner's conditioning experiments showed that the rats could be taught to learn simple concepts and behaviors when they were offered or denied food. From this, Skinner made the almost wholly unsupported inference that human freedom was unnecessary. In books like *Walden Two* and *Beyond Freedom and Dignity*, he suggested that an ideal state would mould its citizens like his rats. Those aspects of society that were least planned, like families and free commerce, would be an impediment to this utopia, and would thus best be eliminated. Where Laing appealed to those who saw themselves as victims of society in need of freedom, Skinner offered validation to radical would-be autocrats and other political extremists opposed to individual liberty. In the strange universe of sixties thought, these readers were frequently one and the same.

The treason of the clerks, part II: There's no villain like the corporate villain

A common theme found in the writings of sixties intellectuals is a visceral contempt for business and industry. The elite children of the 1960s have promoted this idea in movies and television shows that so often feature white male villains heading up giant corporations. It's a safe guess that on-screen CEOs commit murder at roughly 50,000 times the rate they do in real life.

Much of this stems from the influence of two anti-corporate writers: environmentalist Rachel Carson and self-described "consumer advocate" Ralph Nader.

Carson gained fame in 1962 with her publication of *Silent Spring*. A fine writer and a well-trained marine biologist, Carson's work represented the first sustained criticism of the use of pesticides. The book, however, was prone to overstatement and alarmism, especially concerning the use of the pesticide DDT. Carson was right that DDT could be harmful to birds, and that the uncontrolled use of insecticides is dangerous. But Carson's shrill warnings about the dangers pesticides allegedly posed to humans and the environment far exceeded what was supported by science, either at the time or today. In *Silent Spring* she argued that

> the world has heard much of the triumphant war against disease through the control of insect vectors of infection, but it has heard little of the other side of the story—the defeats, the short-lived triumphs that now strongly support the alarming view that the insect enemy has been made actually stronger by our efforts.... Malaria programmes are threatened by resistance among mosquitoes.... Practical advice should be "Spray as little as you possibly can."... Pressure on the pest population should always be as slight as possible.[1]

This advice turned out to be deadly. DDT was banned in various countries based on the kinds of concerns raised by Carson. This led to soaring rates of fatal malaria, which had been contained largely by the effectiveness of DDT in killing malaria-carrying mosquitoes. The result has been the needless death of literally millions of people in Africa and other developing regions.[2]

A more persistent figure in American life is anti-corporate activist Ralph Nader. Nader has long sought out the role of a secular saint. It is an adage that saints are not precisely human, and Nader seems to fit the bill. Neither gay, nor ever married, nor ever known to have had a girlfriend,[3] Nader has made it his life's work to expose corporate wrongdoing. To this end he wrote *Unsafe at Any Speed*. First published in 1965, it was a book-length screed impeaching the safety of General Motors' mid-size Corvair sedan, an unusual rear-engine car. The book cited the car's problems with front-end stability as evidence that GM had knowingly put a singularly dangerous vehicle on the market. Hundreds of thousands of Americans were shocked at GM's alleged greed and callous disregard for drivers' lives. In response to the book, the National Highway Traffic Safety Administration was set up to improve car safety.

> ## If a Republican Said This, He'd Still Be Apologizing
>
> "To put it very simply, he is our first African-American president, or he will be. And we wish him well. But his choice, basically, is whether he is going to be Uncle Sam for this country or Uncle Tom for the giant corporations."
>
> — **Ralph Nader,** speaking on Election Day, 2008, about Barack Obama[4]

Interestingly, in 1972 this agency investigated the book's claims. Its conclusion? The Corvair had an average safety record and was not more dangerous than other cars of its class.[5] Yet, although the book's essential argument was discredited by the very agency set up in response to it, Nader made no apology. Perhaps this is not surprising since Nader is a lawyer, not an engineer or scientist, and his grasp of science is not deep. A liberal magazine editor who had worked with him for years reported that he was against fluoridation of the water supply and thought housecats caused leukemia.[6]

In *Unsafe at Any Speed,* Nader also managed to miss one of the most important changes taking places in the auto industry. He examined the industry when the reliability and cost of American cars, undermined by unionization, was beginning to be challenged by foreign competition. Nader failed to see or talk about this issue, and he subsequently become an activist on behalf of unions, seemingly unaware of the contradiction of being an advocate both for consumers and for the monopolistic unions that have now brought GM and Chrysler to the brink of insolvency. Nader insisted that a government agency was needed to supervise the auto industry and mandate safety features that consumers might foolishly reject, but his distrust of the free market was refuted by later events; the most important safety features introduced in recent years, like airbags, have been demanded by consumers, not by safety agencies. Instead, the government's main accomplishment has been to increase product costs and to create new barriers to entry into the industry.

Nevertheless, Nader has found generous backers for his many institutes and public policy foundations. These make it their business to sue public companies and hector government officials, often for trivial reasons. Having secured this financial support, Nader initiated a campaign against nuclear power—a safe, clean form of energy that emits zero greenhouse gasses. More recently, Nader threw in his lot with teachers unions and emerged as an opponent of school choice. This was, to say the least, an unexpected position to take by someone claiming to be a consumer advocate.

Nader has perhaps earned the most notoriety as a serial candidate for president, having run in every election since 1992, when he was a write-in candidate.[7] In 2000, running as a candidate with something called the Green Party, he performed the difficult task of presenting himself as a bigger leftist than Al Gore. He was rewarded with 2.7 percent of the vote, enough to earn the permanent enmity of many of his fellow ultra-liberals, who blamed Nader for tipping the election to George Bush.

Nevertheless, Nader soldiers on, apparently oblivious to the expiration of his fifteen minutes of fame. He was last heard from when he ran for president again in 2008—and received 0.56 percent of the vote.

Part II

✿ ✿ ✿ ✿ ✿

THE CULTURAL SIXTIES

Chapter Five

☮

ROCK 'N' ROLL: SOUNDTRACK TO THE SIXTIES?

ock music is strongly associated with the 1960s. In movies and documentaries, it often seems that rock music *is* the sixties. This is convenient for buttressing the decade's image as one of youthful, revolutionary ferment. But the truth is that rock music was not as popular as liberals would have you believe. Granted, the Beatles and the Rolling Stones were genuine cultural phenomena who sold enormous numbers of records. So, too, were teen-oriented pop-rock bands like Herman's Hermits and the Monkees. But most of the "seminal" sixties rock bands sold modestly, while many of the most popular performers were crooners, jazz musicians, country singers, and classical musicians.

A quick quiz might be instructive:

Which of the following performers had a number one single during the 1960s?

a) Bob Dylan

b) Jimi Hendrix

c) The Who

d) The Grateful Dead

e) Carlos Santana

f) Buffalo Springfield

Guess What?

❀ Rock music was not particularly popular in the 1960s

❀ Bob Dylan's entire hillbilly persona is phony

❀ More Americans have died of drug overdoses than were killed in Vietnam

g) Jefferson Airplane

h) The Velvet Underground

i) Bobby Vinton

The correct answer is Bobby Vinton alone. Nicknamed the "Polish Prince," Vinton was a popular crooner who scored no fewer than four number one hits in the 1960s. The Who, on the other hand, never had a number one single and only once cracked the top ten. Also topping the charts during that decade were decidedly non-rockin' performers like Staff Sergeant Barry Sadler (for "The Ballad of the Green Beret"), Herb Alpert and the Tijuana Brass, Frank Sinatra, Johnny Mathis, Pat Boone, Steve Lawrence, Louis Armstrong, and waltz conductor Lawrence Welk. Other top-selling artists included Dean Martin, Petula Clark, Paul Anka, Conway Twitty, Roger Miller (country's "King of the Road"), Andy Williams, Henry Mancini, the Singing Nun, Lorne Greene (of TV's *Bonanza*), and Nat King Cole. It was these artists who usually dominated the charts back then.[1] The famed rock producer Clive Davis pointedly noted in his memoirs that when he went to see the Monterey Pop Festival in 1967, rock "wasn't the music of the masses. Not yet."[2]

Our collective memory of what constituted popular music has been skewed. It is true that in 1963 a Beatles' album, *Please Please Me*, went platinum, selling one million copies—a rare feat at the time. But that was also the year when Steve Lawrence's wife, Eydie Gormé, had a platinum record, as did Ray Charles in his country mode, French torch singer Charles Aznavour, country singer Dave Dudley, jazz trumpeter Al Hirt, the New Christy Minstrels, and Andy Williams. Bobby Vinton had two platinum records; Bob Dylan had none.

Music historians tell a different story, however. For example, the *Penguin Guide to Pop Music*, a 600-page encyclopedia, omits an entry for Frederick Loewe, the composer of *My Fair Lady*, one of the biggest selling albums of the decade. Another widely read music history,

Those Wild and Crazy Musicals

Among the biggest-selling albums of the 1960s were soundtracks from Broadway musicals. *The Sound of Music* album was number one on the music charts for twelve weeks, while the movie became the biggest grossing motion picture of the entire decade. Topping the Billboard charts for six weeks, *Camelot* remained on the list for more than five years. *West Side Story* sold an amazing eight million copies by 1970, which was probably more than any recording by any rock band other than the Beatles. *My Fair Lady* was even bigger, ranking as the highest-selling record ever released by Columbia Records before 1970. *Fiddler on the Roof* went platinum and hung on the charts for 187 weeks, while *Mary Poppins* stuck at number one for sixteen weeks and sold six million copies by the end of 1967. The movie *Mary Poppins* was the top-grossing film of 1965.[3]

100 Albums That Changed Music, includes obscure counterculture favorites like Tim Hardin and the Master Musicians of Joujouka, but fails to mention Frank Sinatra.[4]

This isn't just re-writing history, it's gross fraud. To understand what motivates it, we must ask ourselves what rock music really is.

What is rock 'n' roll?

Generally speaking, rock music does not require a lot of talent to play. With a few lessons (and often without them), your average sixteen-year-old can pick up a guitar and churn out a lot of rock classics. In candid moments, even some rock musicians themselves will tell you that rock 'n' roll is just musical fast food. When asked whether rock music was an art form, Kiss singer and bassist Gene Simmons candidly replied,

> None of these guys ever took any music-theory lessons or anything, and that includes me. None of us ever took the time to go to music school, and we can't, to this day, read or write musical notation. We never took music lessons to learn about that. So the deluded notion that we're making anything other than sugar is nuts. I'm not saying that sugar doesn't taste good, but it burns fast. It's not meant to last. This is not classical music. It's modern, popular music, and for somebody who isn't really qualified to call himself a musician to claim he's making art is, at the very least, delusional.... See, the rest of the guys with guitars around their neck want credibility. I don't want credibility. That means nothing. Remember, none of these guys learned how to play their instruments properly. They all did it by ear, the lazy man's out. So a big word like "credibility" coming out of a guy who's unqualified to say anything other than "Do you want fries with that?" is delusional.[5]

To be fair, the 1960s produced a number of talented pop-rock songwriters who could write wonderful melodies, such as Smokey Robinson ("The Tracks of My Tears"), Paul Simon ("Bridge Over Troubled Water"), John Phillips ("California Dreamin'"), Stevie Wonder ("The Tears of a Clown," which was written by Wonder but performed by Smokey Robinson), and most of all, Paul McCartney ("Yesterday"). But to acknowledge a few worthwhile songs does not imply a general endorsement of rock music, just as one can appreciate an excellent TV show while still concluding that the bulk of TV programming is junk. Besides, these songs are actually pop ballads, rather than true rock and roll; they emphasize melody and sentiment, not passion and rhythm.

⊛ ⊛ ⊛ ⊛ ⊛ ⊛ ⊛ ⊛ ⊛ ⊛ ⊛ ⊛ ⊛ ⊛ ⊛

Christian Rock: A Contradiction in Terms?

In 1955 Jerry Lee Lewis was thrown out of a Texas Bible college for playing rock music. Years later, Lewis ran into his old friend, Pearry Green, who asked him, "Are you still playing the devil's music?" Jerry replied, "Yes, I am. But you know it's strange, the same music that they kicked me out of school for is the same kind of music they play in their churches today. The difference is, I know I am playing for the devil and they don't."

The most important source of rock music is the wedding of modern electric instruments with the 12-bar blues music of the Mississippi Delta. Most old-time blues songs were very simple. Like most current pop songs, they typically featured a verse-chorus-verse structure of lyrics. The songs were typically twelve bars in a major key melody, if the song even had a tonic key. When there was a base note—or key—around which the melody was arranged, it was usually a white key on the piano, part of what's called the diatonic scale. The keys with which blues musicians wrote their songs were few, and their experimentation was modest. Their concern was for expressing their moods. This meant developing a style of singing that was near to shouting or wailing and focusing on a solid, driving rhythm in 4/4 time. The favored rhythm of contemporary rock and dance music is this simplest of rhythms.

To make this uncomplicated music more lively and interesting, rock music is spiced up with syncopation. This is a fancy word for music in which some beats in a measure are accented unexpectedly. Syncopation is widely used in jazz and by certain classical composers like Beethoven and Brahms. For them, syncopation is a means to express conflict within their music. The division is eventually resolved at the conclusion of a piece, showing how order can triumph over disorder and beautiful harmony can be rendered out of strife. In rock music, however, syncopation is used to attack the very concept of order. The syncopation doesn't need to be resolved, because the disorder in the accents is the goal and the point of the music, which is aimed more at the loins than at the heart, more at striking adolescent rebellious attitudes than at conveying a sense of aesthetic beauty. The sense of chaos is furthered by the choice of instruments and the style of playing: screeching electric guitars with lots of feedback matched to crashing drums and cymbals.

Mozart insisted that "melody is the essence of music." So what would he make of rock 'n' roll? Here's a hint: he once said, "Music, even in situations of the greatest horror, should never be painful to the ear but should flatter and charm it, and thereby always remain music."

You can decide whether or not Mozart knew more on this point than rock royalty like Ozzy Osbourne. Regardless, the language of rock 'n' roll is telling us a story, one apart from any words that may be attached. The rock music world sees a singer who destroys his guitar on stage or trashes his hotel room as exciting and liberated, not callow, self-indulgent, and vulgar. Sexual freedom and anarchy—passion and disorder—are good, and delicacy, humility, and orderliness are bad.

Anyone who believes this will be apt to regard rock 'n' roll as not only good music, but as an essential statement of values. Is it then so surprising that rock's advocates are determined to write other kinds of music out of history? Or that drug-taking and rock music have always been so keenly intertwined? Or that the most flamboyant rock stars—from Jim Morrison to Sid Vicious—have so often been self-involved sociopaths? Rock music is nihilism in an undiluted form, a pure expression of contempt for authority and convention and a delight in violence and egotism.

"If you go chasing rabbits . . ."

Rock's advocates are right about one thing: rock music was revolutionary and transformative. But its effect was mostly destructive. This is most evident in the intimate relationship that developed between rock music and drugs. Drugs were a crucial part of the sixties counterculture and the rock music scene that propelled it. The promotion of drugs by rock music was—and still is—pervasive, essential, and purposeful. Think of the Beatles' "Lucy in the Sky with Diamonds," the Byrds' "Eight Miles High," Jefferson Airplane's "White Rabbit," the Rolling Stones' "Sister Morphine," Eric Clapton's "Cocaine," Lou Reed's "Heroin," and Bob Dylan's "Rainy Day Women #12 and 35," to name but a few songs. To this day, major record label executives promote drug-tinged bands and songs in order to create a sense of "outlaw" excitement about their acts.

The long list of rock musicians who had drug-related deaths reads like a compendium of sixties rock 'n' roll: Janis Joplin, Keith Moon and John Entwistle (the Who), Jimi Hendrix, Frankie Lymon (the Teenagers), Gram Parsons (the Byrds), Elvis Presley, Brian Jones (the Rolling Stones), Brent Mydland (the Grateful Dead), Ike Turner, Paul Butterfield, Brian Cole (the Association), Gregory Herbert (Blood, Sweat & Tears), Phil Lynott (Thin Lizzy), Bill Murcia (the New York Dolls), David Ruffin (the Temptations), Vinnie Taylor (Sha Na Na), and Alan Wilson (Canned Heat).

The rock 'n' roll lifestyle promoted by the counterculture not only proved destructive for those tragic figures who became addicted to narcotics, but also for many "trippers" who sought out a higher consciousness through psychedelic drugs and rock music. For example, some of the media's favorite sixties characters are Ken Kesey and the Merry Pranksters. The Pranksters took a cross-country bus tour in 1964 to promote the use of LSD, then sponsored a series of parties, the "Acid Tests," in which attendees were encouraged to expand their consciousness by taking LSD and listening to live performances of the Grateful Dead. This

Tune In, Turn On ...
and Become a Fugitive

Alongside rock musicians, one sixties counterculture guru became a key figure in promoting drug use, particularly LSD, among young people—Timothy Leary, coiner of the famous sixties slogan, "tune in, turn on, drop out." A former Harvard psychology professor, Leary is usually portrayed as an avatar, an off-beat and inventive thinker who opened novel paths to understanding by advocating a new youth culture tinged with exotic elements like Eastern philosophy. In reality, Leary was an unabashed conman and advocate of drug abuse. A typical example of his deceitful promotion of LSD is found in his 1966 interview with *Playboy*, in which Leary claimed that "in a carefully prepared, loving LSD session, a woman will inevitably have several hundred orgasms." [6] Among the galaxy of supposed benefits of taking LSD, Leary touted the drug as an effective "cure for homosexuality."[7]

Leary's life largely consisted of a string of publicity stunts. He tried to organize a new religion, with LSD as its most holy sacrament, as a means to gain First Amendment protections for drug use. Always intent on exploiting private moments for publicity and gain, he employed a director from the TV show *Bonanza* to orchestrate his third marriage, where all the guests had taken LSD. In 1996 he undertook his final publicity stunt by having his own death broadcast on the internet.

Leary's life does not seem to have been a happy one—he had four marriages, punctuated by the suicides of his first wife and his daughter. He also had major legal problems: in 1970 he was sentenced to prison on felony drug charges, but he escaped from jail and linked up with the Weatherman terrorist group, which helped him flee to Algeria, where he lived for three years with Eldridge Cleaver and other renegade Black Panthers.[8] He was later extradited back to the United States and served a few years in jail before gaining early release.

Despite his unenviable personal history, Leary became a beloved sixties celebrity, using his academic credentials to provide a veneer of intellectual responsibility to his pro-drug message.

was celebrated in Tom Wolfe's book, *The Electric Kool-Aid Acid Test*, among countless other laudatory chronicles.

In relating the supposed excitement of these events, however, not many sources mention the fate of Sandy Lehmann-Haupt, a sometime driver of the Prankster bus who fell victim to drug-induced anxiety and paranoia, experienced "many lost years," and later condemned the Pranksters for glorifying drugs.[9] A better-known Prankster and sixties icon, Neal Cassady, died within a year of the bus trip, apparently from drug-related causes.

Rock music has been a major cultural driver of drug abuse, leading to the deaths of even more Americans than were lost in Vietnam. According to the Centers for Disease Control and Prevention, just in 2005, 23,618 Americans suffered fatal, accidental drug overdoses.[10] This is nearly half the number of American soldiers killed in the entire Vietnam War. Unintentional drug overdose is now a more common cause of death than suicide or homicide, and it is second only to car accidents among unnatural causes of mortality. It's curious that sixties radicals and their present-day apologists believe the loss of American lives in Vietnam justified violent protest and "acts of resistance" while they simultaneously glamorize the drug culture that has led to a much greater number of deaths.

Bob Dylan vs. Merle Haggard

Bob Dylan, perhaps the first musical phenomenon of the counterculture, is a worthy subject for a book. However, Bob Dylan the "artist" should not properly be the subject. After all, more than almost any other pop culture icon, it's hard to figure out what Bob Dylan's talent is.

Paris Hilton is slim and pretty. Madonna may not sing well, but she can dance—similar to Jennifer Lopez and Paula Abdul. Mick Jagger is an interesting, if weird, stage personality. But what exactly is Dylan's talent? It sure isn't his wretched singing, which Paul McCartney parodied in

"Rocky Racoon" by deliberately singing off-key. Dylan also is a third-rate instrumentalist. He can't even dance. According to contemporaries, Dylan's brother, the record producer David Zimmerman, always played the piano better than Dylan did—and David Zimmerman is six years younger.[11]

Dylan's stage presence is often enervating. Sometimes hostile toward his own audience, he has been booed off the stage more than once. It's said that he is a great songwriter, yet his best-known melodies—"Blowin' In The Wind" and "A Hard Rain's A-Gonna Fall"—were lifted from a spiritual entitled "The Auction Block" and a folk song called "Lord Randall," respectively. (Yes, in the first case, even as Dylan denounced racism, he was pillaging black music.) His lyrics are occasionally somewhat witty—though he is no Cole Porter. His best feature, perhaps, is that he capably plays the blues harmonica, though musicians like Blues Traveler's John Popper play it far better.

Even Dylan's admiring biographers are compelled to admit that his music is exceptionally simple. Nearly all his songs are based on ordinary three-chord progressions, the sort of melodies a beginning guitarist can rapidly pick out with minimal training. Of course, great songs need not be knotty and intricate; stark simplicity can be used to great effect, as in Beethoven's haunting but unadorned piano tune, "Fur Elise." But the primitive form of Dylan's songs is not a choice; it's clear Dylan doesn't know *how* to write complex music. His tuneless songs and affected off-key singing—this is what he can do.

And yet, Dylan has been repeatedly nominated for the Nobel Prize for Literature, while *Time* magazine has named him one of the one hundred most important people of the twentieth century. This begs an important question: why?

Part of the explanation for Dylan's reputed importance may lie in what he does seem to have a talent for: posing. Dylan's favorite persona is that of a poor hillbilly bluesman who speaks from his life of hardship. This would be more compelling had Dylan not grown up in a middle-class family in Minnesota. Born Robert Zimmerman, Dylan came from a Jewish family of shopkeepers and middle-class merchants in the predominantly Catholic town of Hibbing. The Appalachian accent used in his singing is an affectation, since his real voice had a honking Midwestern accent like those in the movie *Fargo*. He had an unremarkable upbringing without any privation; the major events of his teen years were his Bar Mitzvah and his induction into a Jewish fraternity at the University of Minnesota.[12]

Early on, Dylan developed a habit of lying about himself in order to further his career. In his adolescence he was hired briefly as a sideman on a northern swing by the pop singer Bobby Vee. Working under the name Elston Gunn, Dylan hooked himself up by falsely claiming that he'd previously toured with Conway Twitty.[13] He later attempted to escape his first recording contract with Columbia by untruthfully stating that he was underage and that his parents were dead.[14] In 1965 he hid his marriage to former model Sara Lowndes from his assorted mistresses and the press.[15] Perhaps most incredibly, Dylan has invented stories of having worked as a male prostitute.[16]

Nevertheless, his political statements, appearances at civil rights rallies, and ballads sung about civil rights leaders like Medgar Evers served to build up an air of seriousness around him. Yet, in retrospect, Dylan's popularity appears to have a lot in common with that of 1980s hair bands or Madonna. His hats, his shirts, his skinny pants and belts, his many different hairstyles: Dylan was—and is—a master at picking up and discarding clothes and fashion trends in a way that intrigues style-obsessed young people and hipsters of all ages. This impulse for style above substance extends to Dylan's scratchy, off-key singing voice, which is a conscious, phony imitation of the bourbon-soaked voices of old-time bluesmen like Leadbelly. Ironically, its appeal to the young was based on an image of authenticity.

There was a man at the time, however, who had the authentic persona that Dylan faked: Merle Haggard. But the politically incorrect singer could not get the respect of the liberal press. Haggard was a hillbilly Protestant raised in the Scots-Irish ballad tradition, a child of the Dust Bowl migration to California. Haggard's father died when he was nine, after which Haggard fell into truancy and crime. Eventually he wound up serving a sentence in San Quentin, where he saw Johnny Cash perform and befriended the death row inmate Caryl Chessman. His songs about field work, impoverishment, and clashes with the law were drawn from his own life. But once he sang, "If you don't love this country, leave," he forfeited the affections of leftist journalists.

Haggard was a decent, principled man. Although his record company discouraged him from releasing numerous original songs criticizing racism, including one defending an interracial couple, these songs were recorded by others. He was unwilling to pander to the media, however, and therefore never achieved the celebrity of Dylan.

Politically Incorrect Before It Was Cool

Of all Merle Haggard's songs, the most offensive to the Left was "Okie From Muskogee," which was a no-holds-barred attack on the counterculture. Beginning with the line, "We don't smoke marijuana in Muskogee," Haggard ridiculed hippies for their self-indulgent drug-taking, lack of patriotism, and shabby personal appearance. All this he contrasted with the traditional values and flag-waving patriotism of middle America, repeatedly proclaiming, "I'm proud to be an Okie from Muskogee."

Haggard rightfully became a legend of country music—but what journalist writes about or even listens to country? In fact, it's largely forgotten that the 1960s was a great and defining decade of country music, producing million-selling records from performers like Loretta Lynn, George Jones, Glen Campbell, Buck Owens, Ray Price, Waylon Jennings, and Johnny Cash. Of these, the late Johnny Cash is the only artist who receives any media attention, because his well-known drug abuse and womanizing—highlighted in the 2005 biopic, *Walk the Line*—express rock 'n' roll values.

Paul McCartney and George Martin

One rock band of the 1960s stands out, both for its record sales and the quality of its music. However, once more we must note that much of its music *wasn't* rock music.

The Beatles were unusual in that the group included two exceptionally gifted musicians: Paul McCartney, and—no, not John Lennon—producer George Martin. Often called the fifth Beatle, Martin was a remarkable man. Trained as a classical oboist, he eventually rose to the top of the small EMI label, which mixed popular music and comedy with recordings of the baroque repertoire. In this way, he worked both with great cellists and with improvisational comedians like Peter Sellers, Dudley Moore, and Peter Cook. Martin produced and arranged the Beatles' records and even played the piano during their studio sessions. His taste and judgment would be demonstrated after hearing the Beatles' first studio session, when he wisely suggested that Pete Best should be replaced as the band's drummer.[17]

Martin contributed many other crucial concepts to the band. It was his idea, for instance, to turn Paul McCartney's strange, Rachmaninoff-like ballad "Yesterday" into a string quartet. With "Eleanor Rigby," Martin understood that the weird lyrics of alienation were best realized with strings only, and he arranged the piece and conducted it in the style of film score composer Bernard Hermann's music for Alfred Hitchcock films, using none of the Beatles in the playing of the tune. Martin further demonstrated his ingenuity by employing a variety of studio tricks to fit a baroque keyboard line into "In My Life" and to get two vastly different versions of "Strawberry Fields Forever" into synch, producing the song's memorable and eerily disjointed quality. For "Strawberry Fields Forever," Martin also combined one recording with a heavy rock guitar sound with another that he had arranged for cellos and brass. For "In My Life," Martin replaced the usual pop song refrain with a keyboard progression, using studio technology to turn his piano-playing into the sound of a harpsichord by lowering its pitch an octave and changing the speed. On "Penny Lane," Martin found a skilled piccolo trumpet player to play the song's contrapuntal brass melody. For "She's Leaving Home," Martin scored the song for strings and harp, as on other songs he arranged for string octet, sitars, marimbas, and classical church choirs.[18]

If Beatles records don't sound like they have fallen out of a time capsule as most sixties rock does, one big reason is the variety and imagina-

But How Do You Really Feel About It?

"Rock and Roll smells phony and false. It is sung, played, and written for the most part by cretinous goons and by means of its almost imbecilic reiteration, and sly, lewd, in plain fact, dirty lyrics . . . it manages to be the martial music of every sideburned delinquent on the face of the earth . . . . [It] is the most brutal, ugly, desperate, vicious form of expression it has been my misfortune to hear."

— **Frank Sinatra**[19]

tion Martin contributed to the scoring. But McCartney deserves credit as well for his versatility: his "Maxwell's Silver Hammer" sounds like an old English music hall song; "When I'm Sixty-Four," written in the style of the pop tunes from the youth of McCartney's jazz musician father, could easily have been sung by Maurice Chevalier; and "Honey Pie" recalls the Charleston.

While McCartney had numerous hits as a solo artist, he wrote most of his best music with the Beatles. Indeed, it's hard to think of any great Beatles' melody, other than George Harrison's "Here Comes the Sun" or possibly his "Norwegian Wood," that McCartney didn't write. "Hey Jude," "Blackbird," "Let It Be," "And I Love Her," "Yesterday," "Ob La Di Ob La Da (Life Goes On)," "The Long and Winding Road," "When I'm Sixty-Four"—the best melodies are by McCartney, not John Lennon. People remember Lennon's lyrics to songs like "Revolution," "I Am the Walrus," and "Whatever Gets You Through the Night." But let's be honest: these melodies are not particularly creative. Constant repetition is what pounded them into people's heads, so that they're apt to remember them. This was a simple trick Lennon later employed for political effect in his antiwar anthem, "Give Peace a Chance."

Lennon's continued fame derives from his association with McCartney in the Beatles and his image as an intellectual who opposed the war in Vietnam, mocked religion, and claimed that the group was bigger than Jesus. His conflicts with McCartney arose from their differing sensibilities. This was indicative of a difference in values. The melodic pop of McCartney is the voice of love and feeling. The angry, snarling music of Lennon—most evident in songs like "She's So Heavy"—is true rock 'n' roll: the sound of egotism and the unbridled self. Is it any surprise that Lennon was a habitual heroin user and a callous womanizer who humiliated Yoko Ono by making love to a mistress when she was only yards away? This recapitulated Lennon's introduction of Ono to his first wife, Cynthia Lennon: when Cynthia returned from a brief trip abroad, she found her unapologetic husband in her living room with Ono dressed in their matching bathrobes.[20] By contrast, McCartney, who had groupies literally camped out outside his home, by all accounts was a monogamous and loving husband to Linda McCartney, from whom Paul was all but inseparable during their nearly thirty-year marriage, until Linda's death from breast cancer in 1998.

A songwriter's records tell you the record of his soul.

The Rolling Stones

Many of the Beatles' songs promoted drug use—the meaning of "I Get High With a Little Help From My Friends" was not hard to fathom. A bit more obscure was the song "Yellow Submarine," a reference to amphetamine pills that the Beatles liked to swallow before shows.[21] Still, for most of its history, the general image that the band promoted of itself was mostly innocent. Neither early songs like "I Wanna Hold Your Hand" nor later ones like "Hey Jude" are cynical or tawdry, and even songs like "Why Don't We Do It in the Road" were obviously written with tongue placed firmly in cheek.

The Beatles' main rival, the Rolling Stones, present a dramatic contrast and a firmer indication of where popular culture was headed. With albums bearing titles such as *Their Satanic Majesties Request*, *Let It Bleed*, and later, *Sucking in the Seventies*, the Stones aimed to sell records by promoting a mostly accurate image of themselves as debauched and lecherous lowlifes.

This was new.

The Stones made their character clear with the 1965 release of *The Rolling Stones, Now!* The album's jacket-copy instructed fans:

> Cast deep in your pocket for loot to buy this disc of groovies and fancy words. If you don't have bread, see that blind man—

Not Big on Women's Liberation

The Rolling Stones' shockingly demeaning attitude toward women was made abundantly clear in songs like "Brown Sugar," which glorifies Englishmen's rape of black slave girls, and "Under My Thumb," in which Jagger brags that he has taken "the girl who once pushed me around" and turned her into a submissive "squirming dog." Perhaps even worse is "Some Girls," in which Jagger rates the sexual performance of women of various races and baldly proclaims, "Black girls just want to get f****d all night." It's remarkable that self-styled "women's groups" have always given a free pass to the Stones, whose outright misogyny makes Ludacris and other targets of feminist ire look tame by comparison.

knock him on the head, steal his wallet and lo and behold you have the loot if you put in the boot, good. Another one sold![22]

The Stones practiced the kind of anti-social nihilism that they preached. Among their many notorious acts, drummer Brian Jones spiked unsuspecting club-goers' drinks with LSD, and he beat his teenage mistresses until they were bloody. He also posed for photographs in an SS uniform with his foot on the neck of a man posed as an aged Jew. Whether for their camp value, as a means to offend, or in genuine emulation, Nazi themes also appealed to Jagger, who goose-stepped while performing on stage in Berlin. The band also became known for habitually trashing hotel rooms and urinating on the floor of a service station whose owner annoyed them.[23]

For Jagger this created an image of a man possessed by raw, unbridled emotions. But it was not just his liberal employment of eye-shadow and lipstick that showed his lack of authenticity; by his own admission, Jagger's theatrical way of prancing about the stage was imitated from female relatives and Little Richard.[24] This hinted at another aspect of his concealment, one regarding his sexuality. While Jagger deliberately projected androgyny, he sought to conceal the fact that he was carrying on homosexual affairs in addition to his very public trysts with women. Equally fake was Jagger's supposed lower-class origins—he affected a lower-class accent in place of the posh tones he had acquired in his comfortable upbringing and his schooling at the London School of Economics. Fans were led to believe that Jagger was a wonderfully free-spirited and uninhibited "bad boy," but by all accounts he was more preoccupied with money than anything else. He fled England for two years, living in exile to avoid paying British income taxes. He was so concerned for his wealth that he would regularly call his accountants and ask them minute questions about his stream of income, such as weekly sales figures for Stones albums in smaller-market countries like Sweden.[25]

As in so much rock 'n' roll, posturing was more important than, indeed a substitute for, the traditional music talents Jagger lacked—like an aptitude for singing. If Jagger's voice is not as execrable as Dylan's, it is certainly not easily confused with Pavarotti's. As more than a few have noted, Jagger often sounds as if he is talking loudly and drunkenly rather than singing. Was novelist Truman Capote entirely unjust in commenting that "Jagger can't sing, his voice is not in the least charming, [and] he can't dance"?[26]

The Altamont debacle

The Rolling Stones concert in Altamont, California, on December 6, 1969, was a perfect display of the group's nihilistic ethos, serving as a coda for the decade's self-obsessed underbelly of sixties rock.* Organized

* An interesting question is whether or not Jagger—in spite of his academic background—would know what a coda is, since he has no formal musical education and cannot read music.

by the Stones, the concert was intended to rival earlier large rock "happenings" like Woodstock and the Monterey Pop Festival. Jagger hoped that its footage could be rushed out into theaters before the film of Woodstock was released.

In planning the concert, the Stones showed negligible concern for their fans. The group had not even properly arranged a location until two nights before the show; the band axed a plan to hold the concert at Sears Point Raceway in Sonoma after learning it might have to pay a substantial fee and that staging the show there would prevent

> **Rip-off Artists**
>
> "Commercial rock 'n' roll music is a brutalization of the stream of contemporary Negro church music, an obscene looting of a cultural expression."
>
> — **Ralph Ellison**[28]

them from selling lucrative film rights to the concert. Eventually it settled on the Altamont Speedway, east of Oakland, which had been offered for free. Failing to provide adequate portable toilets or emergency medical tents at the site, the Stones were criticized by prominent rock figures, including rock promoter and manager Bill Graham, who warned of the dangerous conditions at Altamont and denounced Jagger's selfishness.[27]

Rather than pay normal security costs for the 300,000 attendees, the Stones hired the Hells Angels biker gang to flank the stage in return for around $500 in beer. This proved disastrous. The Angels' idea of crowd control was to punch people with brass knuckles, beat them with lead-tipped pool cues, and stab them with knives—right in front of the stage. Even the performers were not spared; the Angels assaulted Jefferson Airplane singer Marty Balin after he tried to prevent the bikers from pummeling a member of the crowd.

None of this deterred the Stones. In fact, the group delayed its appearance until after sundown, allowing the scene to grow more rowdy, because Jagger thought his stage make-up looked better at night.[29] The Stones eventually played amidst growing chaos, which culminated when the Angels stabbed to death a young black man, Meredith Hunter, who had brandished a gun. Before the night was over, three other attendees were also killed. Throughout the Rolling Stones performed, providing the filmmakers with the exciting nighttime footage they craved.

After finishing their set, the Stones raced to a helicopter that airlifted them away from the fiasco. Jagger then turned to those present and commented, "That was close. But that's going to make one terrific film." Hours later, back at his hotel room, Jagger pestered groupie Pamela Des Barres to consent to group sex. Ever sensitive, Jagger said that he thought this might help to heal him of the psychic wounds *he* had suffered that day.[30]

Chapter Six

☮

MOVIES AND TV: NOT GREAT, BUT NOT YET DECADENT

There have been great periods in American television; sad to say, the 1960s wasn't one of them. It offered neither the brilliant comedy and live dramas of the 1950s "Golden Age" of television, nor the unconventional and original programming of the last fifteen years. There was no *Your Show of Shows* and no *Seinfeld*, no *Requiem for a Heavyweight* and no *Sopranos*.

Yet, while sixties leftists mock the bourgeois *Ozzie and Harriet* culture that dominated the times, the intellectual level of popular culture then was much higher than it is now. In fact, during the 1960s the networks commissioned serious projects that would never make primetime today, such as a film of Graham Greene's *The Power and The Glory* starring Laurence Olivier, as well as productions of Shakespeare's *Macbeth*, Noel Coward's *Blithe Spirit,* and Arthur Miller's *Death of a Salesman*.[1]

Nor was all the regular programming from the time forgettable. Most beloved today are *Star Trek* and *The Twilight Zone*, but these are hardly the only shows from the period that still delight, intrigue, and move. Episodes of *The Jack Benny Show* and *The Dick Van Dyke Show* continue to amuse, as do many from *The Carol Burnett Show*. Indeed, many comedians insist that these stand up far better than most seasons of *Saturday Night Live*. Even a lot of the 1960s children's shows are still enjoyable, even for adults. Think of *The Addams Family* and *The Flintstones*.

Guess What?

- Popular 1960s TV shows reflected conservative, patriotic values

- The ending of censorship reduced the quality of movies and TV shows

- The highest grossing movie of the 1960s was *The Sound of Music*

Perhaps more important than the quality of sixties TV is what the shows tell us about the culture of the time: that society was still very conservative and polite, but neither static nor incapable of change. Just look at the top-rated shows throughout the decade:

1960–61

1. *Gunsmoke*
2. *Wagon Train*
3. *Have Gun, Will Travel*
4. *The Andy Griffith Show*
5. *The Real McCoys*
6. *Rawhide*
7. *Candid Camera*
8. *The Untouchables*
9. *The Price Is Right*
10. *The Jack Benny Show*

1965–66

1. *Bonanza*
2. *Gomer Pyle, U.S.M.C.*
3. *The Lucy Show*
4. *The Red Skelton Hour*
5. *Batman (Thurs)*
6. *The Andy Griffith Show*
7. *Bewitched*
8. *The Beverly Hillbillies*
9. *Hogan's Heroes*
10. *Batman (Wed)*

1969–1970

1. *Rowan and Martin's Laugh-In*

2. *Gunsmoke*

3. *Bonanza*

4. *Mayberry R.F.D.*

5. *Family Affair*

6. *Here's Lucy*

7. *The Red Skelton Hour*

8. *Marcus Welby, M.D.*

9. *Walt Disney's Wonderful World of Color*

10. *The Doris Day Show*

And here are the next ten ranked shows for 1969–1970:

11. *The Bill Cosby* Show

12. *The Jim Nabors Hour*

13. *The Carol Burnett Show*

Those Were the Days

The show most people associate with the clash between the sixties counterculture and the older generation, *All in the Family*, did not premier until 1971. It is hailed by liberals today as a ground-breaking sitcom that "pushed the envelope" of acceptable fare for TV. In all the praise, however, it's forgotten that what made the show so beloved was the popularity of its main character, Archie Bunker. Although the character was supposed to be an unenlightened, illogical bigot, he became a hero to millions of Americans for his stubborn rejection of the counterculture. It is Archie Bunker's chair that has become one of the most famous exhibits in the Smithsonian's National Museum of American History. Meanwhile, Bunker's counterculture antagonist is now mostly remembered for the derisive nickname Archie gave him: Meathead.

14. *The Dean Martin Show*

15. *My Three Sons*

16. *Ironside*

17. *The Johnny Cash Show*

18. *The Beverly Hillbillies*

19. *Hawaii Five-O*

20. *The Glen Campbell Goodtime Hour*[2]

This list should go a long way toward dispelling the myth that the 1960s was a radical time. Popular American tastes have rarely been so respectable and so respectful of family and country as they were in the 1960s. The dramas and westerns popular then reflected traditional values and strongly emphasized chivalry, duty, and honor.

Westerns and historical adventures were particularly popular during the 1960s. These shows had a ready audience, but they were also put on the air because they were cheaper for the networks to produce than contemporary dramas, which required shooting on city streets. Thus, some of the switchover from westerns to detective shows during the decade reflected a rise in the amount of television advertising. This permitted TV producers to move away from a reliance on back-lots. But there is no doubt that the broad affection of the public for shows like *Bonanza*, *Rawhide*, and *The Adventures of Daniel Boone* demonstrated the depth of the country's patriotism, notwithstanding the clique of Marxist radicals who were causing trouble on some college campuses.

Although sixties TV was certainly tame by today's standards, it did achieve certain landmarks, the most noticeable of which was the advent of color TV. In 1965, *I Spy* became the first show to co-star a black actor (Bill Cosby) and a white one (Robert Culp) on an equal basis. This was followed in 1968 by *Julia*, the first show to feature a black performer in the title role since television's early days of *Beulah* and *Amos 'n' Andy*. Simultaneously, blacks were cast for the first time in parts that did not

TV Censorship: The Good, the Bad, and the Ugly

All TV shows in the 1960s had to send their scripts for approval to censors in the networks' broadcast standards departments. The censors' complaints and demands were often ridiculous. One show that had special problems with the censors was *The Smothers Brothers Comedy Hour*, whose writers included such young talents as Dick Cavett and Steve Martin. On one occasion the show proposed a sketch about censorship: an actor playing a young, love-stricken man is given the line, "My heart is beating wildly in my breast," and a censor changes this to "My pulse is beating wildly in my wrist." Characteristically, network censors rejected this parody of their own work.

Such examples have created the conventional wisdom that censorship brought down the quality of TV during the 1960s. But there is little reason to think this is true. After all, programming quality had been much higher in the 1950s, when censorship was equally if not more strict. A more likely explanation for the fall-off in TV quality during the decade lies with the expansion of the viewing audience. As the number of people with TV sets rose, the pressure on TV writers to dumb down and homogenize their writing grew. Consequently, the most successful TV writers of the 1960s were those who could create cleverly-conceived, two-dimensional characters stuck in off-beat situations, providing engaging but uncomplicated comic material with mass appeal. This approach enriched writer-producers such as Paul Henning *(The Beverly Hillbillies)* and Sherwood Schwartz *(Gilligan's Island* and *The Brady Bunch).*

In fact, the effective end of censorship in television, as in all media, has generally led to declining quality, as concern for writing is replaced with the

continued

continued

preoccupation of finding ways to insert what had once been prohibited—nudity, profanity, and gore—into the scripts. Striking in this regard is the contrast between the campy and harmless *Batman* TV show and the current movie series which, although devoid of sex and nudity, is cynical, sadistic, and filled with despair.

Defenders of the *Batman* movies invariably protest that the movies strive to be not merely "dark" but also "edgy," and that their misanthropy and violence are simply the auxiliary consequences of this. As much better-written material like Rod Serling's *The Twilight Zone* proves, however, dark and provocative material need not be cruel or callous. The current impulse toward presenting scenes of degradation on film and television is motivated by financial and not artistic motives. If Rod Serling were to write a script like *Requiem for a Heavyweight* or Paddy Chayefsky were to pen one like *Marty* today, their subtly drawn characters would likely be of less interest to producers than the need to spice up the scripts with profanity, nudity, or gore so that they matched every other modern film.

specifically call for black actors, such as the Peggy Fair character in the hard-boiled detective series *Mannix*.

Mannix introduced another new development: its starring character was a prototype of the anti-establishment heroes who now dominate popular culture. This shift, meant to make the heroes appear colorful and less beholden to "the man," is worth pondering. Why was this change so universal, and why was it so accepted? The change from John Wayne to Clint Eastwood, from Jack Webb to Steve McQueen, and from Sgt. Friday to Detective Vic Mackey, after all, implies a rejection of authority, tradition, and of the rule of law more broadly.

In the early 1960s such notions were far from the norm. Even the character James Garner played on *Maverick* was intermittently roguish rather than being fundamentally hostile to law and government. Yet scriptwriters and producers today revel in presenting their heroes as anti-establishment anti-heroes who must "break the rules," and audiences are taught uncritically to admire this rebellious quality. It is almost as though we are being told that the existence of laws is a burden, and that we would all be better off in an anarchic state of nature.

Hurray for Hollywood—sort of

From the early 1930s until the mid-1960s, motion pictures were subject to a censorship code known as the Hays Code. By 1967, however, the code had been replaced by the Motion Picture Association of America's rating system, originally consisting of G, M (for mature audiences), R, and X.

As in the television industry, the end of censorship resulted in a lowering of artistic standards in films. Hollywood reps showed no embarrassment in their rush to include irrelevant but titillating sex and violence in their scripts, extolling their new licentiousness as artistic "bravery." Liberal Hollywood insiders in the Academy of Motion Picture Arts and Sciences awarded Oscars to their like-minded colleagues whose films might have been ridiculous, but were sufficiently "transgressive" against social values and the nuclear family. Thus, self-evidently preposterous films like *Who's Afraid of Virginia Woolf?* (1966) and plodding cinematic catastrophes like *Midnight Cowboy* (1969) received multiple Oscars. Incredibly, *Midnight Cowboy* was even awarded the Best Picture Oscar—largely, it would seem, on the basis of the nudity, copious sex, and depictions of gang rape that earned the film an X rating.

This was a dramatic change in Hollywood's conception of itself and its role in society, auguring a trend that has become ever-present: the determination of the movie business to finance "message" movies, even ones without any hope of commercial success, with anti-American, anti-capitalist, anti-religious, anti-family, or antiwar themes.

Throughout the first half of the 1960s, the movie business bestowed its awards on popular family entertainment, giving out Best Picture Oscars to movies such as *My Fair Lady* and *The Sound of Music*. In retrospect, these films have stood up better and seem far less dated than the politically-correct Best Picture nominees that followed, like *The Sand Pebbles* and *Guess Who's Coming to Dinner?* The first of these two films was a ludicrous allegorical melodrama about Vietnam. Telling the story of a disastrous, fictional American naval mission to China in the 1920s, the film aims to show how Western attempts to assist indigenous Asians inevitably fail. The latter film, *Guess Who's Coming To Dinner?*, is an indictment of American racism in which a bigoted couple refuses to accept Sidney Poitier, cast in the role of a brilliant scientist and doctor, as their daughter's spouse because he is black. Shot with the understatement of a howitzer, today it remains affecting and of interest to roughly half a dozen film students.

The cognoscenti also took an interest in several violent movies of the decade that celebrated criminals and criminality, especially *Bonnie and Clyde* (1967) and *The Wild Bunch* (1969). Neither film appealed much to the public, however, and *The Wild Bunch* could even be called a box office flop. Nevertheless, intellectuals were determined to find artistic merit in these movies, to prove that they were "important" and "relevant"—something for which the public was a little too smart.

The taste and sensibility of most Americans can be inferred by looking at the record of what we liked best. The most popular male actor of the decade was John Wayne, and the most popular actress was Julie Andrews. The highest-grossing motion picture was *The Sound of Music*, a film whose success was so huge that adjusted for inflation it remains among the five most popular movies ever made.

While the movie industry touted and honored leftwing piffle, it also produced some memorable comedies, adventures, and thrillers, providing further proof that the film medium is much more suited for these genres than it is for political proselytizing. Consider, for a moment, this brief alphabetical list of clever, lively, and still enjoyable popular films of the 1960s:

Bedazzled (1967)

Cape Fear (1962)

Charade (1963)

Chitty Chitty Bang Bang (1968)

From Russia with Love (1963)

Funny Girl (1968)

A Funny Thing Happened on the Way to the Forum (1966)

Goodbye, Columbus (1969)

The Graduate (1967)

Hello, Dolly! (1969)

The Ipcress File (1965)

Lawrence of Arabia (1962)

Mary Poppins (1964)

The Music Man (1962)

My Fair Lady (1964)

The Odd Couple (1968)

Oliver! (1968)

Paint Your Wagon (1969)

The Pink Panther (1963)

The Producers (1968)

Romeo and Juliet (1968)

Some Like It Hot (1960)

The Sound of Music (1965)

Splendour in the Grass (1961)

The Times, They Are a Changin'

"Despite its supposed raunchiness, the film's tone now seems surprisingly repressed."

—*New York Times* film critic **Janet Maslin**, commenting in 1994 that *Midnight Cowboy*—an X-rated film from 1969 about a man forced into petty crime and gay prostitution and who is victimized in a gang rape—seemed tame by 1990s standards[3]

103

Take the Money and Run (1969)

Tom Jones (1963)

The World of Henry Orient (1964)

This is the legacy that 1960s Hollywood bequeathed to future generations. All told, it's a not a bad record at all. These movies, which simply strived to tell entertaining stories and create interesting characters, have stood the test of time. Movies that preached politics, on the other hand, now seem dated and cliché, as yesterday's burning political issues have given way to new concerns. Likewise, movies that pushed the envelope of sex and violence back then look quaint and ridiculous now, in light of the gasp-inducing sensationalism that pervades movies today.

Foreign films: Trying to make Marxism interesting

Foreign films found a small but growing audience in America during the 1960s. This was the decade of the French "New Wave," and of many of the great films of foreign writer-directors like Federico Fellini, Milos Forman, Akira Kurosawa, Francois Truffaut, Satyajit Ray, Eric Rohmer, Andrzej Wajda, and Ingmar Bergman.

American film critics gave these movies mixed reviews. Unsurprisingly, they were much more enthralled by the movies of two leftwing filmmakers who seemed intent upon inflicting as much suffering as possible upon their audiences: Jean-Luc Godard and Michelangelo Antonioni.

In retrospect, Godard seems a bit like Peter Sellers' character in the movie *Being There*—an empty-headed figure whose extraordinary ability to meet and befriend powerful people and to be in the right place at the right time led him to undeserved fame and fortune. Raised in Switzerland and Paris, Godard was admitted to the Sorbonne in 1948. While hanging out in the Latin Quarter as a university freshman, he became pals with the influential film critic André Bazin, who shared his affection for American gangster films, and the brilliant conservative writer and director Eric Rohmer (*My Night at Maude's*, *Claire's Knee*). Along with Jacques Rivette, they would be among the founding staff of the influential film magazine *Cahiers du Cinema*. Through his work on the magazine, Godard also became closely acquainted with the young François Truffaut, who would ultimately do much—possibly most—of the writing on Godard's first and only good film, *Breathless*, and would introduce Godard to the producer who financed the film, Georges de Beauregard. Perhaps because *Breathless* was essentially light, amoral entertainment— a competent and off-beat variation on an American crime movie—it earned a great reception among French audiences. Brought up on heavily produced studio melodramas from directors like Max Ophüls, Paris found it fresh and fun.

More puzzling was the reaction of American critics who, possibly reading too much into the film's implicit endorsement of its protagonist's casual, larcenous approach to life, hailed the movie as an existentialist masterpiece. In the years that followed, Godard became a committed Maoist, forcing his casts and crews to participate in Maoist self-criticism sessions. The celluloid results were either baffling or interminable. Yet Godard's union of pretentiousness, tedium, and leftwing sanctimony was unbeatable in the eyes of intellectuals.

Godard's mate among overhyped leftist filmmakers was the Italian Marxist Antonioni. A product of the middle classes, Antonioni had this to say about his childhood friendships and romances:

> Our friends were invariably proletarian, and poor: the poor still existed at that time, you recognized them by their clothes. But, even in the way they wore their clothes, there was a fantasy, a frankness that made me prefer them to boys of bourgeois families. I always had sympathy for young women of

working-class families, even later when I attended university: they were more authentic and spontaneous.[4]

Regrettably, the Marxist cant was not limited to Antonioni's interviews. Audiences were subjected to films of 150 minutes or more during which nothing happened, but industrial and bourgeois life were somehow "revealed" as mindless and empty. Often the camera would simply linger on actress Monica Vitti's face and then on a background behind her for unbearably long stretches. In his later films, Antonioni added nudity and sex in a vain attempt to make his dreary nothingness a little more interesting.

By contrast, Eric Rohmer's conservative politics dissuaded critics from acknowledging the depth and brilliance of his intellectual, ironic, and bittersweet comedies. Surprisingly, critics actually voiced some praise for the wonderful anti-Communist and humanist films coming from across the Iron Curtain, movies like Milos Forman's heartbreaking *Loves of a Blonde* and his acidulous allegory, *The Fireman's Ball*. These films, of course, could not be shown in the Communist countries where they were made—a stark reminder of the virtues of Western societies that filmmakers and critics so often took for granted.

Chapter Seven

☮

MODS, MINIS, WIDE TIES, AND BROOKS BROTHERS: THE BEST OF SIXTIES FASHION

Few myths about the 1960s are harder to shake than those about dress. When the producers of the recent movie *Zodiac* screened their film about the late 1960s investigation of a Bay Area serial killer, they were surprised by the reaction to the clothes worn by the film's stars. Why wasn't anyone dressed in Paisley, they were asked. Why weren't the characters wearing tie-dyed vests? Where were the capes and fringed jackets like those seen in *Hair*? Where were the Mod shirts and printed blouses favored by Austin Powers and his Carnaby Street girlfriends?

None of this was in *Zodiac* for a good reason—no one in any ordinary occupation really wore such outlandish clothes at work, not even journalists and not even in San Francisco. As it turns out, the film's costume designers actually made an effort to be accurate, basing the clothing on photographs of what the actual characters and people from the time had worn.[1]

To understand popular clothing of the 1960s, it's important to separate *dress* from *fashion*. Dress is what people wear every day. Fashion is what certain prestige segments of the garment industry promote to attract attention and to create demand for clothes among a limited audience that is preoccupied with novelty and trendiness.

Guess What?

- Sixties fashion was a conservative reaction to the suggestive clothing of the 1950s

- Sixties Hollywood stars were hardly ever photographed in jeans

- The "hippie look" died out almost as soon as it arrived

The dress of the 1960s was very conservative, providing a stark contrast to the overt sexuality of the previous decade. Even student radicals dressed conservatively; if you look at photos of 1960s student protests at Harvard and Columbia, or of marchers heading to the Pentagon, you'll see that the boys are usually dressed in blue blazers or tweed jackets with Oxford button down shirts, regimental ties, and penny loafers, items typically bought at Brooks Brothers, which was the most influential clothier for American men. The young girls wear short dresses with long stockings or woolen skirts—almost never slacks—and unmatched wool sweaters. These sweaters are usually turtle-necks, and they are almost never low cut and rarely tight, as they were in the late 1950s. So even among the most rebellious youth, the dress was far from sexually provocative, reflecting a society that still took formality and propriety in dress seriously.

These customs were even more strictly observed in the workplace and at restaurants and nightclubs. No quality French restaurant or steakhouse in the 1960s would permit a man to dine without a coat and tie. And it wasn't just the finest dining establishments—Lutece and The Four Seasons—that expected decorum from their patrons; all quality restaurants did, even in Los Angeles and San Francisco. Most prestigious private colleges did not permit male students to attend dinner without a tie. Similarly, candidates for political office always wore ties, no matter the temperature outside. Dress at tennis matches was always plain white for the players and respectably preppy among the spectators. Until 1967, the Ascot races did not permit women in slacks, the same policy enforced at many fine restaurants until the 1970s.[2]

In Hollywood, concern for formal dress extended beyond studio luncheons. Movie actors did not appear in public in blue jeans, and studio publicity departments would gladly pay for rented Bentleys from which young stars like George Hamilton were to appear before the cameras wearing double-breasted blazers with white linen slacks. Consider for a

The Mods: It's Not Hip to Be a Hippie

Even before the wild styles of Haight-Ashbury emerged, a fashion revolution had already begun in England.

The Mods were groups of clothes-obsessed young aesthetes. As accurately shown in the film *Quadrophenia*, the Mods often conflicted with so-called "rockers," teens and young men into American greaser styles. Male Mods liked to wear short, trendy suits matched to bushy haircuts and rolled-collar sweaters. Female Mods typically wore mini-skirts with wide belts, shiny knee-length boots or patent-leather shoes, and multi-colored blouses with flouncy sleeves, with their eyes heavily outlined in a Cleopatra-type style.

Overall, the Mods were almost the antithesis of hippies. The Mod style was artificial and calculated. They liked fancy clothes, and they abhorred the ratty leather-jacketed attire of their rocker rivals. Even so, the Mods were pill-poppers, passionate about loud music, and often sexually promiscuous; the term "Swinging London" conveyed an accurate impression of their scene.

But there was not much interest in them outside of London. Hardly any American college students in 1964 were dressing like Mods, no matter that the Moddish Beatles were topping the music charts. In fact, "Swinging London" was barely even noticed by the mainstream in the United States until a *Time* cover story of April 1966. The report came the same year as the release of the Michael Caine film *Alfie*, which detailed the misadventures of a caddish cockney taking advantage of the city's loosened sexual mores.

moment that it's hard to find a picture of Warren Beatty out of costume before 1967 in anything except a three-piece suit.

As an expression of the day had it among studio executives, "Dress British, think Yiddish."

While the dress of the 1960s was generally conservative and often notably sexless, the decade witnessed the emergence of youth fashion as an independent market and a strong influence on fashion sensibilities. Until the 1960s, fashion was something that really referred to the money spent by mature women on expensive clothes appropriate to their married lifestyles. Young American women did not go to or look to French Haute Couture design houses for clothes, and the classic dressmakers did not look to them for ideas. Dressmakers like Richard James and Cristobal Balenciaga produced elegant, floor-length outfits for women aged thirty and older.

Yet by the 1960s rising levels of disposable income were creating a separate youth culture that was expressed in fashion as well as music. This first became clearly noticeable in England, where the Teddy Boy fashion emerged in the 1950s, running on into the early 1960s.

The Teddy Boys were few in number, but they attracted a lot of attention. Mostly working-class, they showed up at London nightclubs wearing old-fashioned frock coats with wide lapels and ruffled shirts. The general claim is that they wore these clothes with a sneering sense of irony, and that they really had contempt for the portion of the British aristocracy and the upper middle-class that had once worn frockcoats. It seems more likely, though, that they simply enjoyed the theatrical appeal of the clothes. Either way, the Teddy Boys introduced a new mode of dress that may not have lasted long, but presaged the later trend that fashion would cater to the young.

Jackie and Audrey: Adult fashions

The fashions of the 1960s can be divided into two chronological periods. The first style wave ran roughly through 1966. During this time, beehive hairdos were in vogue, and elegant, "modern" styles predominated. The major influences on women's fashions were Jackie Kennedy and Audrey Hepburn, and their respective principal designers, Oleg Cassini and Hubert de Givenchy. The First Lady famously favored pillbox hats, long white gloves, boxy suits, and sleeveless A-line dresses worn with a minimum of jewelry. Cassini later claimed that he had

The Mini: Nice Dress You're Almost Wearing

Sixties fashion is closely associated with the advent of the miniskirt and the form-fitting bra. Many commentators attribute the popularity of these accessories to the sexual revolution. As noted earlier, however, there was no sexual revolution in the 1960s. The real cause of the trend towards the mini and the form-fitting bra is simpler: technology.

British designer Mary Quant had been making and selling mini-skirts from the beginning of the Kennedy presidency. In the early 1960s, some women had worn miniskirts with old-fashioned silk or fine wool stockings that ran almost to the knees—most of us today associate this "vintage" look with the decade. But, as the style was neither practical nor seemly, the mini only really took off with the simultaneous rise of pantyhose in the mid-1960s.

While the mini is often said to represent the "sexiness" of the 1960s, it emphasized youth much more than sex appeal. The styles of the 1950s—tight sweaters, slimming girdles for the waist, high heels, and exaggerated curves—were much more sexual. This can also be seen in the switch away from heavy underwire bras toward more natural form-fitting bras using stretch fabrics like Lycra. These so-called "elastomerics" bras from makers like Playtex and Marks and Spencer provided a more comfortable but less feminine profile, and their popularity coincided with the sixties vogue for androgynous, almost child-like models like Twiggy and Jean Shrimpton. As the 1960s wore on, less bosomy and more gamine film stars like Audrey Hepburn, Julie Christie, and Jane Fonda took the place of 1950s sexpots like Jayne Mansfield and Marilyn Monroe.

designed almost three hundred outfits worn by the First Lady during her less than three-year stay at the White House.

The rage for Jackie, or "Jacqui" as the French called her, cannot be underestimated. Her ecstatic greetings from Parisian mobs screaming "Vive Jacqui!" were among the great celebrity excitations of the century. Less widely discussed but equally startling was the reaction she provoked on a tour of India, a trip for which the First Lady took forty-eight pairs of gloves: her crowds exceeded those of Queen Elizabeth, and the press and the public both referred to her as "Amerika Maharani"—the American Queen. Polls from 1961–66 ranked her as the most admired woman in the nation. Her TV special, "A Tour of the White House," was a phenomenon, seen by 80 million people and distributed to 106 countries. Manufacturers worked triple-shifts to meet the demand for copies of her pill-box hats. When she wore a leopard-skin coat, the price of leopard-skin coats shot up seven times and the animal was placed on the endangered species list.[3]

This mania continued even following her husband's death. Jackie Kennedy was put on the cover of an average of thirty-five magazines a month between 1963 and 1966. This included three *Life* and three *Look* covers when she was no longer First Lady. Most important, while Jackie's style affected the whole range of ages, it was strongest upon women in their teens and twenties—girls in high school, college, and in their first jobs.[4]

Audrey Hepburn's image was only slightly less powerful. Although her figure was slimmer and more elegant than the First Lady's, Hepburn's manner was anything but aggressively sexual. In movies like *Breakfast at Tiffany's* she popularized a look featuring men's button-down shirts, Capri pants, ballet flats, and full-skirts with cinched waists. Again, this was a reaction *against* the more sexual 1950s style, one that was underlined by her preference for short hair. The choice of Hepburn for the lead in *Breakfast at Tiffany's* indicates the extent to which blaring sex appeal had lost its luster. Author Truman Capote desired Marilyn Monroe for the role, and readers of the novella will recognize that Monroe was far closer to the part, that of a hick and a kept woman. Keenly focused on the box office, however, the producers insisted on the more up-to-date Hepburn.

Hepburn and Kennedy's influence on fashion was strongest in the early 1960s, before young people began strongly influencing fashion. Sorority girls sought out Jackie's pill-box hats and Hepburn's cloches, and adolescent girls still regularly looked for fashion cues to much older society women like the Duchess of Windsor, C. Z. Guest, and Babe Paley. That young people were following their elders can be seen in the popularity among young women of full-length "Oriental" silk dresses and of the low, sleek, unadorned heels that Jackie Kennedy preferred. These were not the styles of the girls on *American Bandstand*. Moreover, as leisure time activity increased, skiing and traveling to historic sites and to national parks grew in popularity. Consequently, ski-wear sales shot up and middle-class men bought increasing numbers of short "car coats." People in their thirties weren't trying to look younger; young people were trying to look older. Indeed, one of the most noticeable fashions among young men in the early 1960s was pipe-smoking.

Alas, all good things must come to an end. Later in the decade the younger generation began staking its own claims to fashion. In this, as in so many other areas, sixties youth would have been better off listening to their parents. It's unlikely that many parents in the 1960s were later embarrassed by what they wore during that decade. The same cannot be said for a certain subset of the younger generation out in California.

Haight-Ashbury: Where good fashion went to die

San Francisco's Haight-Ashbury district is a section of old Victorian bungalows located somewhat to the west of the city's fancy Nob Hill district and just south of the beautiful Golden Gate Park, which adjoins the bridge and the Bay. During the 1950s the district fell into decline, and most of its ornately detailed private homes were broken up into cheap apartments. The low cost of the area made it an enclave for drop-outs and self-proclaimed artists, an association furthered when a number of Beat poets took up residence there.

It has never, however, produced any writers, painters, poets, sculptors, or artists of the first rank. The Beat poets identified with the area, like Lawrence Ferlinghetti, fall more into the category of self-professed poets than candidates for the Nobel Prize, and what talent the Haight-Ashbury "scene" may have offered the world consistently burned out quickly. Typically, Haight-Ashbury resident and novelist Ken Kesey couldn't write a word worth reading after the publication of the uneven 1964 novel, *Sometimes a Great Notion*.

This pattern of unfulfilled promise was also evident among the neighborhood's pop musicians. The best-known of these was the vastly overrated Janis Joplin, a heroin-addicted singer with a screechy off-key voice who died of a drug overdose at age 27. Among Joplin's peers in the local music scene was Jefferson Airplane. The band produced a few memorably weird compositions like "White Rabbit" and "Somebody to Love," then promptly ran out of ideas and repositioned themselves for the mass-market with trite, annoying pop songs. The focus on these later albums seemed to be on the logo design and t-shirt sales, yet the group continued to denounce multinational corporations and consumerism while serving both.

The same pattern applied with somewhat less shamelessness for the Haight's most popular band, The Grateful Dead. The Dead, of course,

That's One Way to Put It

Offended by Jefferson Airplane's commercialism, leftwing rock critic Lester Bangs described the band as "radical dilettante capitalist pigs."[5]

became the most popular "acid rock" band of all time, a group whose fans turned up regularly across the country for their marathon jam-session concerts. The group's fans particularly appreciated that alone among popular bands the Dead allowed concert-goers to tape their shows. This was hailed as proof of the band's noncommercial, communal bona fides. Another view would be that this was simply a clever marketing ploy by which the band gained ticket and merchandise sales. That the band's hostility to money was in some measure an act may be indicated by its behavior at the Monterey Pop Festival: while they loudly proclaimed that they'd only perform if the concert's proceeds went to charity, once the promoters agreed, band members refused to sign film and record releases for their performances.[6] In later years the band's leader, Jerry Garcia, supplemented his wealth from the band's fantastically successful merchandise sales by offering his own line of neckties to bourgeois office workers.

The Dead's drug-fuelled concerts unarguably had wide appeal. The quality of the band's songs is another matter, though. Hardly anyone in pop music seems to think enough of these to re-record them anymore, and any judgment of the Dead must concede that Garcia's talents as a guitarist were necessarily limited by the missing middle finger on his right hand.

So if Haight-Ashbury failed to offer up much in terms of music or art, what was its real influence? Well, if it has a real claim to fame, it is this: the district spawned the modes of dress that most of us think of when we hear the term "hippie." Closely associated with the psychedelic drug culture, the style spilled out beyond the Bay area and began influencing wider popular fashion at the very end of the decade. Tie-dyed patterns, loud floral prints, bell-bottomed pants, and long, flowing dresses gained a certain cachet among the counterculture youth. The clothing sometimes became sexually suggestive, with low-cut halter tops becoming a popular accessory.

Still, the trend toward wild or risqué clothing never really gained currency in most of the country. What's more, the hippie look died out almost as soon as it arrived. The style was aesthetically ridiculous, with bell bottoms and other fashion travesties of the time providing fodder for Denis Leary and countless other stand-up comics to this day. But more important, the style had trouble surviving outside the psychedelic drug culture that produced it. This culture was self-destructive and unsustainable, leaving a trail of devastation most starkly symbolized by the fate of Haight-Ashbury itself. Once a lovely Bay Area neighborhood, the district became overrun with thousands of drug-addicted, psychologically damaged youths—so-called "waste cases" who populated the area's mental hospitals, lived on the streets, or otherwise existed as wards of society. In the end, the hippie fashion was ugly, as were the consequences of the hippie lifestyle.

Chapter Eight

☮

TO THE MOON,
BUT AT WHAT PRICE?

*I*f one iconic moment emerged from the 1960s, it was man's first steps on the moon. The Apollo 11 mission was celebrated as a monumental accomplishment in the history of not only America, but of all humanity. An estimated half a billion people—then the largest television audience for a live event, ever—tuned in on July 20, 1969, to watch Neil Armstrong take one giant leap for mankind as he stepped down from the *Eagle* lunar module onto the moon's surface. The feat was widely hailed as the achievement of the century.

But what exactly is meant by "achievement?" Unlike the synthesizing of pharmaceutical penicillin, manned moon missions saved no lives. Unlike the fighting of the Korean War, they rescued no nation or people from oppression. While they did advance our understanding of geology and astronomy, these bits of scientific knowledge could not possibly justify the missions' fantastic expense. After all, the purpose of landing a man on the moon was never to learn something; it was just to prove we could do it. No other space mission would be "more impressive to mankind," President Kennedy vowed.

One element of the mission that was truly astronomical was the price, which was widely estimated at $40 billion,[1] or $232 billion when adjusted for inflation. Other estimates run as high as $100 billion, or $581 billion in today's dollars.[2] To get some perspective, the higher estimate is

Guess What?

❧ The United States never fell behind the Soviets in space technology

❧ Johnson, Kennedy, and Nixon all hyped the Soviet space threat for political gain

❧ Manned moon flights were a costly, futile boondoggle

almost half the cost of the Vietnam War. Even the lower figure as a proportion of GDP is about what the United States has spent so far on the Iraq War. For this sum, subway systems could have been built for every large American city, or the whole of college and graduate school tuition could have been paid for millions of young people.

The Apollo moon landings may have looked like stunning "achievements" at the time, but in retrospect they seem like something else: overpriced publicity stunts.

The politics of outer space

Politics, of course, was a big factor in the decision to fund the Apollo program, geared toward setting a man on the moon. This goal was first announced in 1961 by President Kennedy, who had warned during his presidential campaign of a "missile gap" between the United States and the Soviet Union. This played off fears stemming from the Soviets' successful 1957 launch of *Sputnik 1*, the first satellite to orbit the Earth. The Soviets were winning the "space race," Americans were warned, and we'd better do whatever it takes to catch up and overtake them.

There was much less to the space race than met the eye, however, and in fact there was no race at all to place a man on the moon, since the Soviet Union had no realistic program to do so. What's more, notwithstanding Kennedy's claims, the United States had never fallen behind the Soviets in rocket or satellite technology. That the Soviets beat the United States in launching a satellite reflected a conscious decision by President Eisenhower. Although Ike wanted to launch satellites to spy on the USSR, he worried that satellite reconnaissance might contradict some aspects of international law. Therefore, to avoid Soviet-orchestrated international protests, he allowed the Soviets to launch a satellite first. Eisenhower's thinking was justified; based on U-2 spy flights, he knew the United States had a giant lead in the technological development of military satellites, rockets, and intercontinental ballistic missiles. Consequently, he repeatedly rejected calls to expand the U.S. space program as needless and wasteful.[3]

But the supposed inferiority of America's space program became the subject of hysterical ranting by media outlets like *Newsweek* and by all the top candidates to succeed Eisenhower as president—Kennedy, Lyndon Johnson, and even Eisenhower's own vice president, Richard Nixon. The alarmism was pure politics; both Kennedy and Nixon intimated, either privately or publicly, that moon missions would serve no practical function.[4]

But both men were competing politically with Lyndon Johnson, then Senate Majority Leader, who was particularly apoplectic in whipping up fear that we were vulnerable in space. "Soon [the Soviets] will be dropping bombs on us from space like kids dropping rocks onto cars from freeway overpasses," Johnson warned darkly.[5]

In reality, the supposed Soviet foothold in space mostly consisted of putting small dogs into squat metal containers that were shot up into high altitude—sometimes accidentally killing the dogs in the process. Shooting a doomed puppy into space, however, was not nearly as useful or advanced as the

A Warning Unheeded

There is considerable evidence that when Eisenhower warned in his farewell address of the dangers of the "military-industrial complex," he was concerned as much with the costs of space exploration as with regular military contracting.[6]

space technology the United States was developing at the time, such as intricate weather tracking systems and maritime global positioning systems. Unknown to the public, by August 24, 1960, a U.S. satellite had yielded pictures of 1.5 million square feet of Soviet territory, including detailed photographs of "sixty-four airfields, twenty-six surface-to air missile sites, and a major rocket launch facility." In days, the satellite had picked up more information than had been gained in years of U-2 flights. The Soviets had no comparable surveillance capabilities.[7]

Nevertheless, Johnson decried the space gap as a matter of national urgency. As he explained to a credulous public and a lazy and gullible press, "Control of space means control of the world, far more certainly, far more totally than any control that has ever or could ever be achieved by weapons, or troops of occupation. Whoever gains that ultimate position gains control, total control, over the Earth, for the purposes of tyranny or for the service of freedom."[8]

This demagoguery was far more ludicrous than anything Joseph McCarthy had said during his hearings on Communist subversion. After all, Communists really had gained influence in the State Department, they really had stolen secrets for developing atomic bombs, they really were organizing in Hollywood and in labor unions, and their spies like Harry Dexter White and Alger Hiss really had advised presidents Roosevelt and Truman. (Consider for a moment that the notorious Communist theoretician Herbert Marcuse was *openly* serving in the State Department in the late 1940s as its director of policy coordination for Central Europe.) McCarthy may have exaggerated the threat, but at least he was addressing a genuine problem. The specter of Soviet space-based domination of the United States, on the other hand, was pure fantasy.

Nevertheless, the political pressure became too great on Eisenhower, who in 1958 signed off on a Congressional bill to create a separate agency for space exploration, NASA. The scientists on Eisenhower's own six-man advisory committee warned that the United States was embarking on a "complex and costly adventure," noting that

> among the major reasons for attending the manned exploration
> of space are emotional compulsions and national aspirations.
> These are not subjects which can be discussed on technical
> grounds. However, it can be asked whether the presence of a

man adds to the variety or quality of the observations which can be made from unmanned vehicles, in short whether there is a scientific justification to include men in space vehicles.[9]

Such sentiments were even shared by the first head of NASA, Keith Glennan, who told Eisenhower that if the United States should "fail to place a man on the Moon before twenty years from now, nothing will be lost."[10]

Such sober guidance, however, became lost in the panicked insistence that we were losing the space race. And so manned moon missions went forward, without any real justification other than the need to "do something" to beat the Soviets.

One giant boondoggle for mankind

NASA established Project Mercury to put Americans into orbit around Earth. The project proceeded even though President Kennedy's scientific advisors offered the same advice as their predecessors had given Eisenhower: don't focus on manned spaceflight. "Stop advertising MERCURY as our major objective in space activities," the advisors counseled, adding, "Indeed, we should make an effort to diminish the significance of this program to its proper proportion before the public, both at home and abroad. We should find effective means to make people appreciate the cultural, public service and military importance of space activities other than space travel."[11]

Although Project Mercury successfully put a man into orbit in 1962, NASA never adequately explained what was so important about manned space flights. Unmanned flights can achieve most of the things a manned flight can at far less effort and cost. Manned flights have to return to Earth, so the rockets must be much larger, more complex, and more powerful. Additionally, the men require oxygen, complex fire extinguishing systems, special food and the means to ingest it, heating and ventilation suits, mechanisms for bodily excretion while in their space suits, extra room, devices to communicate with Earth and with each other, and a means to resist intense g-forces.

One small example is indicative of the complications of manned space exploration: to appease the astronauts and make them feel like they were really "pilots," at great expense NASA added to its spacecraft high density windows designed to withstand incredible friction, temperature changes, and barometric pressure shifts—even though the windows contributed nothing to scientific understanding. Each window had to be bolted with super-strength materials and tested in thousands of extreme conditions. Then the interior of the spacecraft had to be redesigned to deal with the temperature changes produced by the introduction of light, and further tests had to be done to insure the pilots' safety when they were confronted by light that had not passed through the screen of the upper atmosphere.[12]

Even the term "pilot" was misleading when applied to the initial astronauts, who were little more than passive observers locked inside rockets that were controlled from below. As Tom Wolfe remarked, "What was most required was a man whose talent was for *doing nothing* under stress." He further noted that most conventional aircraft pilots viewed the astronauts as nothing more than "spam in a can."[13] In fact, the National Research Council in 1960 described the Mercury Project astronaut as "a redundant component" in a system in which no one on board has "to turn a hand."

Yet when legendary test pilot Chuck Yeager made the same point in an interview, reporters chose not to divulge his remarks.[14] The bulk of the press, having enthusiastically jumped on board the space bandwagon, didn't like airing criticism of the "heroes" of such a magnificent endeavor. Similarly, hardly any politicians had the courage to question what exactly we were getting in return for such an expensive vanity project. (Barry Goldwater and Gerald Ford were among the very few skeptics, to their lasting credit.)

Another problematic aspect of the space program was the participation of Nazi war criminals in Project Mercury and the Apollo missions. Most notorious was chief rocket engineer Wernher von Braun, whose later insistence that he was forced to join the Nazi Party runs up against a wall of facts as long as the path to the lunar landscape: from 1933 he was a member of the National Socialist Aviation club, and he took membership in an "SS-horse-riding club, a Nazi-affiliated trade union, a hunting club, a welfare organization, and a National Socialist air raid protection corps."[16] The V-2 rockets von Braun designed for the Nazis were manufactured by slave laborers brought from concentration camps and literally worked to death. It is clear that von Braun knew this all along, because his brother Marcus provided him constant, detailed, on-site reports from the manufacturing plants.[17] What's more, von Braun admitted that he personally went to the Buchenwald concentration camp to get "more qualified detainees," as he put it.[18] Another early NASA engineer, Arthur Rudolph, was a former Nazi Party member who superintended the Dora concentration camp, where thousands of inmates were tortured and hanged.[19]

At the end of World War II, von Braun, Rudolph, and a group of about one hundred other Nazi engineers packed up their blueprints, research

Race-based in Space

The Apollo program became the focus of an early effort at affirmative action when the Kennedy Administration tried to force NASA to take on a black astronaut, Ed Dwight, who had far less experience piloting high-performance jets than his white counterparts. The effort, however, was sunk by Chuck Yeager, who was in charge of the trainees and showed a commendable unwillingness to cut corners.[15]

papers, materiel, spare parts, and stocks of rockets, and turned it all over to the United States in exchange for permission to emigrate to America. The decision to head *en bloc* to the United States was practical; the engineers correctly surmised that the United States would provide not only safe harbor from anti-Nazi reprisals by the Soviets and others, but the opportunity for continued employment and generous funding as well. For many years after the war, U.S. rocket testing was almost exclusively carried out with V-2s—the rocket developed and used by the Nazis—that these Nazi engineers provided. Under Operation Paperclip, their personal histories were deliberately obscured, they were given U.S. citizenship, and many ultimately found their way to NASA.[20]

A Book You're Not Supposed to Read

The Right Stuff by Tom Wolfe (NY: Bantam Books, 2001)

The Soviets also employed former Nazis, though they were much lower-level scientists than von Braun and his ilk. Lacking top German engineers, the Soviet rocket program proved relatively primitive, experiencing numerous major setbacks, including a July 3, 1969, launch that exploded 600 feet from the ground, and another launch two years later that blew up after 57 seconds. A 1972 launch lasted just 107 seconds before all six of the rocket's engines failed.[21] Even at the end of the Communist regime in 1991, the Russians still hadn't mastered liquid hydrogen fuel, meaning their rockets relied on propulsion from less powerful propellants like kerosene and liquid oxygen. Both Soviet and American officials, however, exaggerated the occasional Soviet success while downplaying or ignoring their myriad failures, many of which the Soviets kept secret. There was a lot of publicity when the Soviets hit the moon with an unmanned rocket in 1959, for example, but much less attention surrounding the five failed attempts that preceded it.

The moon landings did not lead to countless new inventions

Among NASA's most frequent justifications for the Apollo Project was that the resulting "pure science" would more than pay for itself. When very few discoveries resulted from the moon landings, though, the agency's boosters bizarrely began giving NASA credit for discovering materials like Teflon and Velcro that had actually been around for decades. And even if they had been telling the truth, would the supposed invention of Teflon really justify the billions of dollars and millions of man-hours spent to send men to the moon? Was all that really necessary in order to find a better way to fry bacon?

What did develop from NASA research was the bar code scanner, which was needed because there were so many parts required in the assembly of a Saturn rocket—over three million—that no existing inventory system could keep track of them. This was symbolic of the giganticism that quickly became a primary characteristic of the entire Apollo program: the vehicle assembly building in Cape Canaveral was fifty-two stories high and the biggest building on earth by volume;[22] the crawler-transporter that dragged the rocket's sections to the launch pad was the largest land vehicle on the planet, so heavy that it required 100-foot causeways with a foundation of gravel seven feet deep; and it took 800,000 workers to build the multi-stage rocket.[23]

The fantastic price and scope of the space program, in fact, guaranteed its perpetuation to this very day. Once begun, the project was so enormous that it developed its own political constituency that benefitted from it. Most notably, factories and research centers were placed in politically important congressional districts across the country. Mission Control went to Johnson's home state of Texas, and much of the key engineering design work was parceled out to companies in Kennedy's native Massachusetts.

Indeed, the Apollo Project quickly turned into a colossal public works program, enabled only through the activities of millions of taxpayers who provided the money to finance this historic boondoggle—and received hardly anything in return.

Except, allegedly, Teflon.

Part III

❀ ❀ ❀ ❀ ❀

THE POLITICAL SIXTIES

Chapter Nine

THE UNWARRANTED COURT: EARL WARREN AND HIS BATTLE AGAINST THE CONSTITUTION

During the 1960s, decades-old laws dealing with criminal justice, freedom of religious expression, private property, free enterprise, and public morality were rescinded. This trend, revolutionary in many ways, had begun in the 1950s but was strongly propelled forward in the 1960s. It did not stem from a shift in the population's mood, as the people were not even consulted on these changes and their elected representatives had no say in the matter. Instead, American society was fundamentally refashioned through the diktats of the Supreme Court.

The Court did not always play such a crucial role in American life. For most of our history, the key issues facing America were decided by our elected representatives, from local officials and state legislators up through congressmen, senators, and the president. Before the Civil War, the Supreme Court only overturned two acts of Congress; between the war's end and the 1950s, it still acted with great restraint, only overturning laws when Congress had clearly contravened the Constitution.

During the Warren Court, however, nine unelected justices laid claim to vast new powers, ushering in the current system of judicial supremacy. The Warren Court dates to the 1950s, but it really came into its own in the 1960s, when it issued numerous radical rulings that upended the

Guess What?

- Earl Warren, a liberal icon, championed Japanese internment

- The most radical political effects of the 1960s were achieved through judicial fiat

- The Warren Court was stained by corruption

previous balance of powers between the legislative, executive, and judicial branches. This undeclared revolution was led by one man: Earl Warren.

Who was Earl Warren?

Warren was an intellectual in the worst sense of the word. While he conversed intelligently about broad policy issues, he was impersonal and strangely lacking in normal human feelings. This aspect of his character was revealed way back when he ran for California attorney general in 1938. In the midst of his campaign, Warren's father Methias was found murdered in his ramshackle Bakersfield home, having been beaten with a lead pipe. Police suspected a recent prison parolee who had passed through the area before being sent back to jail. Lacking any proof, the police sought to place a stool pigeon in the suspect's cell to try to record a confession. As a kind of formality, the police asked for Earl Warren's consent to the plan. They were stunned when Warren objected to the practice of secret taping—even to discover who had beaten his own father to death.[1]

Warren won his campaign and four years later was elected California governor. Although a Republican, Warren's ideology was marked primarily by an abiding faith in the wisdom and necessity of big, coercive government. This was most evident in Warren's assumption of the leading role in adopting and implementing Japanese internment policies during World War II. While today internment is almost always attributed to President Roosevelt, it's largely forgotten that he and many other powerful politicians initially opposed internment, with FDR deriding even the suggestion of firing Japanese workers as being "as stupid as it was unjust."[2] But Warren, then California attorney general, played the key role in getting the policy approved. He had maps drawn up showing "Jap" land holdings along the West Coast, then made elaborate demonstrations to reporters showing how close the "Nips" were to railroads, ports, oil

☮ ☮ ☮ ☮ ☮ ☮ ☮ ☮ ☮ ☮ ☮ ☮ ☮ ☮

The Unremembered Warren

Earl Warren has become a liberal icon, but his attitudes toward Japanese-Americans during World War II were hardly "progressive." Here are a few of his statements:

- "When we are dealing with the Caucasian race, we have methods that will test the loyalty of them...when we deal with the Japanese we are in an entirely different field and we cannot form any opinion that we believe to be sound."[4]
- "The consensus of opinion among the law officers of this state is that there is more potential danger from the Japanese born in this country than from the Japanese born in Japan."[5]
- "The only reason we haven't had disaster in California is because it has been timed for a different date, and if we don't do something about it, it is going to mean disaster both for California and for the nation...we are approaching an invisible deadline."[6]
- "[If the Japanese were released from internment camps], no one will be able to tell a saboteur from any other Jap...no more dangerous step could be taken."[7]

depots, military bases, and other points vulnerable to sabotage. Warren concluded that "the Japanese population of California is, as a whole, ideally situated...to carry into execution a tremendous program of sabotage on a mass scale."[3]

As governor, Warren continued to demonstrate a blind faith in big government, becoming the first elected governor in U.S. history to propose compulsory health insurance. His scheme, which was defeated in the legislature, would have forced nearly all state residents into one health plan while giving state government bureaucrats the power to set hospital and doctor fees.[8] Warren also pushed for—and won—dramatic increases in various tax rates, including a doubling of the state gas tax.

But perhaps Warren's most important decision, at least for his own future, was to support Dwight Eisenhower's 1952 presidential campaign. In return for helping to deliver California's electoral votes, a grateful Eisenhower in 1953 rewarded Warren with a fateful appointment to the Supreme Court.

Power grab: The Warren Court in action

Warren's tenure on the high court can be roughly divided into two parts: 1953–1961 and 1961–1969. During the first period, the Court made several controversial rulings that significantly expanded judicial power. The most famous of these, the 1954 *Brown v. Board of Education* decision outlawing segregated schools, is celebrated by liberals as a tremendous blow for equality. In *Brown*, the Court set out to determine if the passage in 1868 of the Fourteenth Amendment, with its equal protection clause, was designed to outlaw segregated schools. The Court's finding that segregated schools were inherently unequal was unarguably true, and the decision abolished a major injustice in American society.

Nevertheless, the Court showed an ominous willingness to ignore the Constitution and legislate from the bench. Since the Fourteenth Amendment clearly was not designed to outlaw segregated schools, the Court's decision relied on extremely dubious pop psychology research asserting that black children's stated preferences for a white doll over a black doll supposedly proved that segregation caused "confusion" in black children's self-conceptions.[9]

More important in some ways was a follow-up ruling in 1955. Known as *Brown II*, this decision gave federal courts—not Congress—the authority to issue writs to implement school desegregation. At this time,

Congress wished to avoid taking any action in the controversial matter, and the country's intellectuals supported *Brown*. Therefore, few among America's political elite objected to this radical expansion of judicial authority. This ruling, in fact, was the origin of many subsequent judicial outrages involving busing, environmental regulation, and countless other areas in which courts now invent new laws, first usurping the role of legislators and then assuming an executive function in managing implementation of their own rulings.

Having thus set the stage for judicial supremacy, the Warren Court lost all sense of restraint in the 1960s, laying claim to unprecedented powers that have yet to be negated. It all began with two little-noticed cases. In the first, *Mapp v. Ohio* (1961), the Court held that evidence in a criminal case must be excluded if obtained without a valid search warrant. Years earlier the great jurist Benjamin Cardozo had addressed the question, wondering why "the criminal is to go free because the constable has blundered." Weren't police departments separately charged with the duty to take action in response to their officers' ineptitude or overzealousness? As in *Brown*, however, the Court seized for itself the power to dictate answers to problems in other branches of government.

Not Liked by Ike

In retirement, Dwight Eisenhower was asked by a reporter if he had made any mistakes as president. "Two," Ike replied. "They are both on the Supreme Court." He meant Earl Warren and William Brennan.[10]

The second case was *Brown Shoe Co. v. United States* (1962), in which the Court came to the baffling conclusion that the merger of two shoe companies would lead to an illegal monopoly—even though their combined market share of domestic production and sales were 4 percent and 2 percent, respectively.[11]

Having established that it knew far more about police procedures and economic competition than the mere prosecutors and economists who testified in the *Mapp* and *Brown Shoe Co.* cases, the Warren Court really hit the accelerator with the *Engel v. Vitale* case. This 1962 case stemmed from a challenge to a New York state law that permitted the following prayer in the state's public schools: "Almighty God, we acknowledge our dependence upon Thee, and we beg Thy blessings upon us, our parents, our teachers and our country." The prayer was nondenominational and its recitation was voluntary, yet the Court struck it down as a violation of the First Amendment's establishment clause. The clause, of course, prohibits *Congress* from establishing a religion, without placing any such restriction on state legislatures, many of which had official churches when the Constitution was ratified. But the court no longer felt restrained by the mere words of the Constitution or by judicial precedent. And it was just getting warmed up.

In *Gideon v. Wainwright* (1963), the court established the novel legal principle known as *substantive* due process. While the idea of due process has always included the right to counsel, the Court expanded this right by ruling that a poor person is entitled to free counsel if he cannot afford an attorney. Since this was already the practice in all but five states, the decision hardly addressed some urgent national need. What's more, it was constitutionally suspect; as critics like Judge Robert Bork have pointed out, it is rather strange to suggest that the founding fathers did not fully understand a central concept like due process, given that most of the founders routinely tried cases themselves—and none ever commented on the need for uniformly available, federally compelled legal counsel to the indigent.[12]

A parade of even more perverse rulings was still to come:

Katzenbach v. McClung (1964): A small barbecue restaurant in Alabama wanted to serve whites only. As the restaurant used some products from out of state, the court ruled that its activities fell under the federal government's right to regulate interstate commerce. Therefore, the restaurant was commanded to be integrated and to employ black workers under the Civil Rights Act of 1964. Like the *Brown* decisions, the court used a worthy goal—desegregation—to mask a shocking legal ruling, this one severely diminishing private property rights by effectively asserting that all commercial activity is subject to the government's authority to "regulate" interstate commerce. As a standard liberal law textbook acknowledges, "A fair reading of the opinion seems to indicate an almost unlimited power in any area Congress can claim to fall within its commerce authority."[13]

Griswold v. Connecticut (1965): The Court abruptly discovered that the Ninth Amendment includes a special right to purchase condoms, which until this ruling had been illegal in the Nutmeg State. In dissent, Justice Potter Stewart made the obvious observation that just because a law was "uncommonly silly" did not mean the Court had the authority to strike it down.

A Book Named "John Cleland's Memoirs of a Woman of Pleasure" v. Massachusetts (1966): The Court found that porn novels

Private Property: Nice, but Not Necessary

"It's not necessary to go into the basic questions raised by Black."

—**Justice Goldberg's** response during deliberations in the Katzenbach case after Justice Black asked whether property rights needed to be protected.[14]

are covered by the First Amendment and struck down laws prohibiting them. One wonders how and why it was that the founding fathers were unaware of this and why they passed so many obscenity laws in their state legislatures. This was the first of a string of judicial rulings that led to the birth of the modern porn industry, thereby providing government-approved employment to grateful pimps, madams, and hustlers.

Miranda v. Arizona (1966): Warren and four concurring justices composed a majority that found that a rapist-murderer who freely confessed to his crime had to be released because he was not apprised of his right to a lawyer before he was questioned. Instead of defending his decision with his usual reference to invented rights that are unmentioned in the Constitution, Warren plainly admitted that his aim was to prevent coercive police interrogation methods—methods that, in fact, had already been banned.

The effects of this ruling have been devastating. According to the National Center for Policy Analysis:

> After the *Miranda* decision: The fraction of suspects questioned who confessed dropped from 49 percent to 14 percent in New York. In Pittsburgh, the confession rate fell from 48 percent to 29 percent....Following the decision, the rates of violent crimes solved by police fell dramatically, from 60 percent or more to about 45 percent, where they have remained.
>
> The rates of property crimes solved by police also dropped.
>
> With fewer confessions and fewer crimes solved, there were also fewer convictions....This means that each year there are 28,000 fewer convictions for violent crimes, 79,000 fewer for property crimes and 500,000 fewer for other crimes....[But] even the Court agreed that genuinely coerced confessions were rare at the time of *Miranda*.[15]

Warren stepped down from the court in 1969, but his cohort continued his legacy into the 1970s, issuing a series of radical decisions designed to re-order American society. These included:

Griggs vs. Duke Power (1971): After high school-educated black employees of a utility sued because they were allegedly being denied promotions, the Court ruled that job requirements have to be eliminated unless a company can prove they aren't discriminatory. At the same time, the Court summarily banned employers' use of IQ tests in hiring and promotion. Eventually, this ruling also led to prohibitions on employers' examining high school transcripts. As with *Miranda,* this decision had a long string of toxic effects, including a wave of frivolous but costly job discrimination lawsuits, huge increases in the cost of doing business, increasing rates of reverse discrimination in the workplace, and the wholesale devaluation of high school grades and high school degrees.

New York Times v. United States (the "Pentagon Papers case") (1971): Former National Security Council aide Daniel Ellsberg leaked a classified Defense Department study of the Vietnam War to the *New York Times* and the *Washington Post*. The papers, hoping to undermine public support for a war they opposed, indicated they would publish the document. The Nixon administration sued to stop publication, arguing that the leak would weaken the position of U.S. negotiators at the Paris Peace talks. The Court ruled 6–3 in favor of the *Times*, making the untenable argument that the First Amendment protected a newspaper's right to publish government secrets during wartime.

Objectivity? Who Needs It?

The *New York Times*'s reporter on the Pentagon Papers story, Neil Sheehan, later spent eighteen years writing *A Bright Shining Lie*, a 700-page attack on the Vietnam War.

Most critics of the ruling focused on national security, asking how a government can capably function in wartime—or at anytime—if newspapers are allowed to print government secrets. There is, though, another troubling dimension to the decision. The Pentagon Papers were government property of which the *Times* was making unauthorized wholesale use. If the government does not have the right to protect its own property, what is to stop people from stealing from a shed in a public park or claiming other public properties as their own? There is a clear line from this ruling to later rulings permitting vagrants—on spurious First Amendment claims—to sleep in bus depots, train stations, and other public places, regardless of the threat they may pose to passers-by.

Furman v. Georgia (1972): In overturning the death sentence against three black men convicted for rape and murder, the Court passed dramatic new restrictions on the use of capital punishment. Showcasing the court's typical penetrating insight, Justice William O. Douglas found it was particularly immoral to end the lives of criminals who had done poorly in school.

Roe v. Wade (1973): In a 7–2 decision, the Court found that women have the absolute right to abort an unborn baby during the first trimester of pregnancy (when the baby supposedly cannot survive outside the womb), a right to abortion in the second trimester with certain restrictions, and a right to abortion in the third trimester in order to preserve the mother's life or health. The Court based its ruling on a constitutional right to privacy, even as it admitted that "the Constitution does not explicitly mention any right of privacy."

The ruling did not detail the medical degrees and licenses of its authors because they possessed none. More important, they failed to acknowledge that technological progress might later allow babies to survive outside the womb at an earlier point than the justices identified. This, in fact, is what is happening, but the ruling survives even after its core assumptions have vanished.

> ⊕ ⊕ ⊕ ⊕ ⊕ ⊕ ⊕ ⊕ ⊕ ⊕
>
> ## Aside from That, the Ruling Is Solid
>
> "One of the most curious things about *Roe* is that, behind its own verbal smoke-screen, the substantive judgment on which it rests is nowhere to be found."
>
> —Harvard Law School professor **Lawrence Tribe**, one of the most influential American liberal legal scholars

Power corrupts

How has all this happened? How has the one branch of government that is not directly accountable to the people been allowed to seize so much power? Some blame surely lies with the mass media, which has continually failed to report the Court's grasping rulings as the judicial usurpations that they are. The media really has no excuse, since judges themselves have recognized the Supreme Court's slow-rolling coup d'etat since the early days of the Warren Court. After Supreme Court justice Sherman Minton retired in 1956, for example, he ruefully remarked that Justice Goldberg, Warren's most loyal ally, was "a walking Constitutional Convention."[16] Another Supreme Court justice, Felix Frankfurter, had warned in the mid-1950s that "it is nothing new for lawyers to identify desire with constitutionality and to look to the Court to declare unconstitutional legislation one does not like.... The so-called liberals...now want to strike down all legislation that touches civil liberties."[17]

But surely most of the blame lay with judges who cannot resist the temptations of power or the urge to ingratiate themselves with the press and the liberal Washington establishment. These temptations are enhanced when they are not men of character, and several of the Warren Court members were not. The Court's most radical justice, Abe Fortas, committed numerous improprieties, most notably his acceptance while serving on the Court of a secret $20,000 per year payment, which was fixed to transfer to his widow after his death. The money was provided by Louis Wolfson, a known stock swindler who eventually served time in federal prison. While a sitting judge, Fortas also received a large, unannounced honorarium from his former law firm, which had cases pending before the Court.

Furthermore, Fortas repeatedly lied in sworn testimony to the Senate during hearings to consider his promotion to chief justice. His denial that he had met with or advised the Johnson administration while on the Court was complete fiction as Fortas, a former Johnson aide, had consulted with his old boss and with members of the administration dozens of times on a wide range of issues, including government appointments, urban rioting, and the prosecution of the Vietnam War. Fortas had even helped draft presidential statements. Yet he flatly denied all this under oath.[18] After his corruption became public knowledge, Fortas resigned from the Court in disgrace.

Another reliable Warren ally, Justice William O. Douglas, also furtively went on the payroll of a suspicious character, in this case Albert Parvin, owner of the Flamingo casino in Las Vegas and business associate of notorious mobster Meyer Lansky. Parvin had been named as a co-conspirator with Wolfson, Fortas's benefactor, in the securities fraud case that led to Wolfson's conviction. Yet Douglas was simultaneously the supervising judge for the part of the country that includes Las Vegas.[19] Douglas used Parvin's payments to fund divorce settlements to his three ex-wives, one of whom Douglas repeatedly locked up and physically abused. (But maybe it was a fair fight, since she was *forty years* younger than he.)[20] Moreover, his intellect was not much higher than his moral standing; in *Sierra Club v. Morton* (1972), Douglas pronounced that trees and other "inanimate objects" should have standing to sue in federal court.[21]

These were the kinds of people who engineered a stealth revolution in America, using the courts as a tool for arbitrarily overthrowing decades of legal precedents. It is one of the most dramatic and long-lasting consequences of the 1960s, one that was a purely top-down enterprise engineered by a stunningly small clique of unelected radicals. While many of the trends, ideas, and policies that emerged in the 1960s had only a fleeting existence, Earl Warren's invention of the activist court thus far has proven irreversible.

Chapter Ten

☮

CAMELOT AS IT REALLY WAS

*J*ohn F. Kennedy has become a liberal icon. Widely regarded as a martyr for progressive ideas, his administration is now hailed as "Camelot," a magical time when America was embarking on an uplifting new path, led by a young, charismatic president.

This emotional remembrance of the Kennedy presidency continues even though every aspect of it has proven false. Far from the energetic, vigorous president recalled today, Kennedy was a physically debilitated man suffering from a stunning array of serious disabilities. Moreover, his emergence as a liberal saint is hard to square with his actual policies, especially his die-hard anti-Communism and his affinity for low taxes.

The story of Kennedy's presidency has to begin with this: Kennedy's election came about through one of the greatest confidence acts in American history. Camelot, in fact, was a stolen castle.

The 1960 presidential race was one of the closest in history. Nationally, only about 100,000 recorded votes separated Kennedy and Nixon out of almost 69 million cast. In the popular vote, this was proportionately closer than any other election of the twentieth century, and was even closer than George W. Bush's razor-thin victory over Al Gore in 2000.

Kennedy's "victory," however, was a fraud. His election relied on the late appearance of masses of ballots that gained close victories for

Guess What:

- ✌ John F. Kennedy and Lyndon Johnson gained their biggest political victories through vote fraud

- ✌ Kennedy deceived the public about the pitiful state of his health

- ✌ Radical students' political hero, Che Guevara, advocated atomic war (as did Fidel Castro)

141

Kennedy in Illinois and Texas. Had these two states gone to Vice President Nixon, Nixon would have won.

Vote fraud in Illinois, where Kennedy won by just 9,000 votes, was particularly egregious. The corruption of the Chicago Democratic machine was so notorious that in the early morning following Election Day, when it became apparent that the *New York Times*'s presumptuous announcement of Kennedy's victory might be wrong, *Times* managing editor Turner Catledge began hoping that Chicago Democratic mayor Richard Daley Sr. would steal the election for Kennedy simply so the paper wouldn't be embarrassed.[1]

Catledge would not be disappointed.

Daley had abundant reason to make sure Kennedy won—considerations that went far beyond partisanship or his old ties to Kennedy's father, Joe. Daley's primary concern was ensuring that Republican state attorney general Benjamin Adamkowski, who was investigating corruption in Daley's political machine, would lose his re-election bid. In a city known for party-line voting, this meant that Nixon had to lose as well, so that the results wouldn't yield a suspicious number of split tickets showing Democratic votes for attorney general and Republican votes for president.

The early returns suggested a close victory for both Nixon and Adamkowski. Around midnight Kennedy's brother-in-law, Illinoisan Sargent Shriver, went to his room to cry when he realized that the Illinois results would likely tip the presidency to Nixon. Then, Shriver received a sudden bit of unexpected good news: the late votes from Chicago were showing unprecedented Democratic majorities.

Later, when independent prosecutor and long-time Democrat Morris Wexler was appointed to investigate the Chicago results, he returned 667 charges of vote fraud against the Daley machine. And though a Daley loyalist dismissed most of these charges, three Daley politicos eventually pled guilty to perpetrating the fraud, while an election judge in the city's 27th ward publicly acknowledged seeing the theft take place. In one precinct of that ward, the 376 registered voters cast 397 votes. Another precinct had only 22 registered voters, yet official results showed Kennedy beating Nixon there 74 to 3. Moreover, more than 8,000 extra Adamkowski votes were later uncovered during a partial—but quashed—Republican recount.[2]

It was vote theft on an amazing scale. Journalist Earl Mazo, sent by the *New York Herald Tribune* to investigate, discovered one outrage after another. Mazo learned of a cemetery where every tombstone had produced a voter, and he found a vacant,

> ## Bring Out Yer Dead!
>
> It is said that every journalist knows two things about Chicago elections: that Chicagoans vote early and often, and that the dead can be counted on to turn out.

boarded-up house that was listed as the official residence of fifty-six voters in a ward whose results came in late for Kennedy.[3] Incredibly, Chicago's official voter turnout dwarfed the national average, 89 percent to 63 percent.[4]

Fraud of this scale placed Kennedy and Daley in debt to many unsavory figures. One of these was Thomas Kluczynski, the Daley machine judge who dismissed Wexler's charges against Daley's cronies. A year later Kennedy appointed Kluczynski to a federal judgeship.[5] Kennedy also prevented any federal inquiries into the fraud by appointing his brother Bobby as United States Attorney General.

One consequence of this cover-up was that election fraud continued unabated in Chicago, with obvious cases of vote fraud being reported in the 1968 and 1972 elections.[6] As shown by the 2009 indictment of Governor Rod Blagojevich on corruption charges, old habits die hard in Illinois politics.

With a little help from his friends

Results in many parts of Texas were equally absurd. Kennedy's running mate was Lyndon Johnson, head of the Texas Democratic machine. Johnson was already practiced in the art of pilfering elections, as demonstrated in his election to the United States Senate in 1948.

The Democratic primary for that election had, in effect, taken place twice. First, Johnson lost an open primary to former governor Coke Stevenson by more than 70,000 votes. This result came despite a massive campaign of vote fraud by Johnson's camp. Johnson arranged for poll watchers to be seated where they could not see the counting, and his aides had local police arrest uncooperative election observers.[7] Many counties reported outrageous, Stalinesque results, such as Duval County, where Johnson officially beat Stevenson by 3,707 votes to sixty-six.[8] It was not for nothing that the future president earned the nickname "Landslide Lyndon."

Such tactics kept Stevenson from reaching 40 percent of the total vote, the threshold needed to avoid a run-off election. So the top two candidates, Johnson and Stevenson, faced off again. And Johnson wasn't about to lose.

In the run-off, Duval County again reported preposterous results: 4,195 votes for Johnson, thirty-eight for Stevenson. But Johnson was still several hundred votes behind. So the next night Duval suddenly discovered an extra ballot box which came in 425 for Johnson, two for Stevenson. A historian later sardonically noted the county's "astonishing display of civil responsibility," as exemplified in its improbable 99.6 percent official voter turnout.[9]

But six days after Election Day Stevenson was still a few votes ahead. By then, it hardly came as a surprise when Johnson's men miraculously found scores more Johnson votes.[10] A key Johnson enforcer, Luis "Indio" Salas, later admitted to the Associated Press that votes had been made up wholesale, with ballot records showing lists of voters who had supposedly voted in alphabetical order.[11] Court testimony revealed that Johnson aides had called district officials in San Antonio and other areas to request that extra votes be "found."[12] Even Johnson's ally, future governor John Connally, later conceded that this was an unprecedented theft of a Texas election.[13]

So Johnson was an experienced vote thief by 1960, when he presided over an even more fraudulent campaign to deliver the Texas vote to the Kennedy-Johnson ticket, for now Johnson controlled the political apparatus of the whole state. As the *Washington Post* later noted, "In Fannin County, which had 4,895 registered voters, 6,138 votes were cast, three-quarters of them for Kennedy. In one precinct of Angelia County, 86 people voted and the final tally was 147 for Kennedy, 24 for Nixon."[14] Even in sparsely-populated counties, the results came in hours late, often showing huge majorities for the Democrats.

Richard Nixon showed immense unselfishness and decency as the White House was swiped from him. In December 1960, a few weeks after conceding the race, he called Earl Mazo, the reporter covering the vote fraud scandal for the *New York Herald-Tribune*. Off the record, Nixon confirmed to Mazo that he'd probably been cheated of victory. But Nixon also asked Mazo to stop writing about it. A patriot, Nixon argued that Mazo's articles were casting doubt on the legitimacy of Kennedy's victory at a time when the Cold War necessitated solid presidential leadership. Thus, media coverage of Kennedy and Johnson's ill-won campaign came to end—at Nixon's insistence.[15]

Viva la resistance—to Communism

As Nixon indicated, the Cold War dominated the foreign policy challenges of the Kennedy administration. The primary challenge for

Kennedy was Cuba, where rebels had seized control of the island and were converting it into a giant Communist prison camp.

Kennedy deserves credit for recognizing the repugnant nature of Cuban Communism. This was a sharp contrast to the position of many on the left who were enamored by the Cuban revolution and its charismatic leaders, Fidel Castro and Ernesto "Che" Guevara.

Foremost among Castro's early promoters and supporters was the *New York Times*.[16] When *Times* reporter Herbert Matthews met Castro in 1957, Castro was hiding out in the Sierra Maestra mountains after his guerrilla

Herbert Matthews: Useful Idiot Extraordinaire

In writing about Castro, *New York Times* reporter Herbert Matthews sounded like a star-struck schoolgirl. Here's how he first described the guerilla leader for American readers: "Taking him as one would at first, by his physique and personality, this was quite a man—a powerful six-footer, olive-skinned, full-faced, with a straggly beard. He was dressed in an olive-gray fatigue uniform and carried a rifle with a telescopic sight, of which he was very proud....The personality of the man is overpowering. It is easy to see that his men adored him and also to see why he has caught the imagination of the youth of Cuba all over the island...a man of ideals, of courage, and of remarkable qualities of leadership."[19]

Matthews' fawning accounts later became a source of embarrassment for the *New York Times*, whose publisher, Arthur Hays Sulzberger, admitted Matthews had "misled" readers and shown "poor judgment." *National Review* magazine had some fun at the *Times*'s expense, running a cartoon showing Castro exclaiming, "I got my job through The *New York Times*."

army had suffered a series of devastating defeats by Cuban government troops. Short of money and food, Castro had just a handful of fighters left.[17] Matthews, though, portrayed Castro as the triumphant leader of "hundreds of highly respected citizens" in a movement that was "radical, democratic and therefore anti-Communist."[18] Matthews' adulatory account helped to mythologize Castro, opening up a flow of radical-chic funds to help rebuild Castro's broken army.

Matthews' instincts could not have been more wrong. The man he praised as a brave anti-Communist went on to establish a bloody Communist dictatorship marked by secret police squads, the execution of thousands of political prisoners, and the imprisonment of hundreds of thousands for "crimes" ranging from criticizing Castro's leadership to mere suspicion of being homosexual. Torture in Cuba's political prisons became routine, including forced starvation, beating with paddles, and electroshock treatment. Castro's Communist economic policies moved Cuba from having the highest per capita GDP in the Caribbean to the lowest. Western media accounts tend to portray Castro as an ascetic, but he has sixty homes and was estimated in 2005 by *Forbes* magazine to be the seventh richest world leader, with a fortune of $900 million. Until recently, women were kept constantly available by the state security services to serve as his concubines.[20]

Revisionist historians argue that American hostility pushed Castro into Communism—even though as early as 1959 Castro's air force chief, Pedro Luis Diaz Lanz, one of his oldest comrades, defected to America

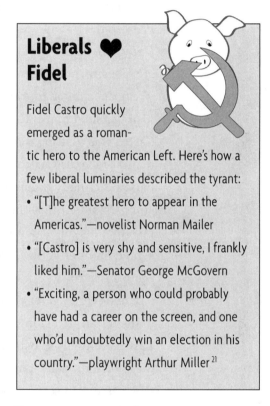

Liberals ♥ Fidel

Fidel Castro quickly emerged as a romantic hero to the American Left. Here's how a few liberal luminaries described the tyrant:

- "[T]he greatest hero to appear in the Americas."—novelist Norman Mailer
- "[Castro] is very shy and sensitive, I frankly liked him."—Senator George McGovern
- "Exciting, a person who could probably have had a career on the screen, and one who'd undoubtedly win an election in his country."—playwright Arthur Miller[21]

and testified to Congress that Castro had told him of his plans to eliminate private banks and set up a Soviet-style system.[22] America's supposed hostile response to all this was for the State Department to arrange for millions of dollars in special loans to Cuba. When Castro visited America in 1959, he met with madly supportive crowds at New York's Central Park, the National Press Club, the United Nations, Yale, and Harvard. At Princeton, students carried him on their shoulders, giving him, as the *Daily Princetonian* put it, "a riotous welcome," part of "a festive crazy atmosphere, bubbling with enthusiasm."[23]

On the campaign trail, Kennedy didn't believe the hype. In fact, he distinguished himself as an outspoken critic of the increasing repression Castro was visiting on his own people. In the last weeks of the presidential race, as Castro positioned Cuba as a Soviet-allied Communist nation, Kennedy began to call for military action. He even accused outgoing President Eisenhower of permitting a Communist government to take root "eight jet minutes from the coast of Florida."[24] Kennedy also signed an open letter supporting Cuban émigrés who were organizing against Castro.

Unknown to voters at the time, Eisenhower was already drawing up plans for an invasion by anti-Communist Cuban émigrés to overthrow Castro. Kennedy's rival for president, Vice President Nixon, knew about these secret plans but could not reveal them. Kennedy thus managed to make Nixon look weak on Cuba, a view furthered by former president Truman, who declared during the campaign, "If we had anybody [in the Eisenhower administration] with guts, we wouldn't be in this situation."[25] As one leading historian noted, Kennedy's "promise to deal severely with Fidel Castro may have made the difference with voters in the South and the Midwest who were otherwise suspicious of his Catholicism."[26]

And so Kennedy, with the help of deceased Chicago voters, was elected. Ten days later, he was briefed by the CIA on the active Cuban invasion plan. The CIA stressed the need for swift and "overwhelming" action in light of the steady stream of Soviet arms shipments to Cuba.

This was where Kennedy's actions failed to match his uncompromising campaign rhetoric. The Eisenhower plan called for a massive American air attack to provide cover for invading Cuban émigrés. But Kennedy feared that robust U.S. air support might produce civilian casualties that would provoke a Soviet military response against West Berlin—never mind Soviet leaders were not exactly famous for their humanitarian concern for foreign civilians. So he scaled back the planned air support, deciding it could only come two days after the invasion began. Delaying air support, Kennedy hoped, would fool the world into thinking the invasion had not been coordinated by the United States.

Simply put, Kennedy lacked courage. He had campaigned as an anti-Castro hardliner, but he was reluctant to withstand the political heat that overthrowing the dictator would generate. His solution was simply to dump the émigré fighters onto Cuba. If they won, he could take credit. If they lost, he hoped to have plausible deniability—laughable as such denials would prove.

Just days before the invasion the landing site was switched to the Bay of Pigs, an area rich in coral reefs that impeded the émigrés' arrival. Moreover, the landings took place without a planned diversionary landing in

Communism: Making Slavery Look Good by Comparison

Today, the average Cuban eats about a fourth as much meat and substantially less rice, bread, and beans than slaves on the island did in the 1840s.[27]

another location. This led to the disastrous capture of nearly all 1,200 men who had set out believing America would provide air cover and possibly troops to support them.

The Bay of Pigs was Kennedy's first major foreign policy test, and the President failed miserably.

Peace through superior firepower

Castro's victory reinforced the Soviets' perception of Kennedy as a weak-kneed pushover. Despite Kennedy's tough campaign rhetoric, the Soviets had reason to hope for his victory over Nixon in 1960. Nixon had gained a strong reputation through his famous "kitchen debate" with Soviet premier Nikita Khrushchev at the 1959 American National Exhibit in Moscow. Showing perfect cordiality and liberally praising Khrushchev and the Soviet Union, Nixon cleverly and subtly demonstrated the absurdity of the Soviet leader's rejection of the right to free expression. Nixon also used his surroundings, which showcased modern American home appliances, to demonstrate American technological superiority. Khrushchev saw Nixon for what he was: steely and capable, a man not to be underestimated.

The Soviets' view of Kennedy was altogether different. He was seen as a pretty boy, an effete product of great wealth, a novice and a lightweight. In Castro's charming words, Kennedy was an "illiterate millionaire" and an "imbecile and a cowardly and despicable, miserable dog."[28] Kennedy's reputation for weakness and indecision was cemented by a string of failures early in his presidency: the Bay of Pigs disaster; his 1961 summit with Khrushchev in Vienna (the pair's first direct meeting, after which Kennedy himself acknowledged that Khrushchev had pushed him around); and his meek acquiescence later that year to the building of the Berlin Wall.

Kennedy's perceived weakness emboldened the Communists to take their biggest gamble of the entire Cold War—the installation of offensive nuclear weapons in Cuba. First detected by American U2 reconnaissance planes on October 15, 1962, the missiles would be capable of striking American cities within

A Book You're Not Supposed to Read

Against All Hope: A Memoir of Life in Castro's Gulag by Armando Valladares (New York: Encounter Books, 2001).

minutes, possibly destroying America's principal communications systems even before retaliatory air force squadrons could get off the ground.

Textbooks today often aver that Kennedy showed steely guts and determination by ordering a naval blockade to keep Soviet missiles from reaching Cuba, and that he did it in order to defend the United States. In fact, American officials were less worried about the missiles' destructive capabilities than they were that their installation in Cuba would embolden world Communism. Historian Robert E. Quirk remarks of the CIA's advice to Kennedy during the Cuban Missile Crisis:

> The analysts saw the Soviets' major objective in Cuba as the need to demonstrate that the world balance of forces had shifted in their favor. The missile bases would prove that the United States could no longer stymie the expansion of Soviet power, even into the Western Hemisphere. American acquiescence in the installation of strategic missiles on the island, they maintained, would provide encouragement for anti-American sectors in Latin America, with a consequent "serious decline" in American influence.[29]

This advice, along with an earlier CIA report predicting that a naval blockade would not provoke war, "provided the rationale for Kennedy's decision to confront the Soviets directly and his subsequent refusal to back down in the face of counterthreats."[30] Kennedy rightly feared a loss of confidence in America's leadership of the free world.

Moreover, the United States did not win the crisis solely due to Kennedy's grit, though he showed plenty of it. The blockade worked because the United States was playing poker while holding nearly all the high cards—it had the best, the most, and the newest weapons.

A Soviet defector, Colonel Oleg Penkovsky, had provided the United States government extensive information on Soviet missile forces indicating that America had a huge lead in armaments. America possessed 27,297 nuclear bombs with more than 200 intercontinental ballistic missiles (ICBMs) to deliver them, most of which could be launched from hardened, underground silos. In comparison, the Soviets had just 3,332 nukes and only a handful of ICBMs. These typically had just over half the range of American ICBMs, and had to be launched from exposed surface launchers. Similarly, American nuclear submarines could fire without surfacing, while Soviet subs could only fire after surfacing and

Che: The World's Most Popular Genocidal Maniac

Che Guevara has become the ultimate radical chic fashion accessory, with his face emblazoned on the t-shirts of thousands of naïve college students and would-be radicals around the world. A key fighter in Castro's revolution and a fanatical Communist, Che is romanticized by many leftwing historians today as a wonderful humanitarian motivated by his love for all people, a view shamelessly propagated in the 2008 movie *Che*, starring Benicio Del Toro.

In truth, Che organized Cuba's labor camp system and personally executed people deemed to be enemies of the revolution.[32] He was a dogmatic Communist ideologue motivated by a utopian desire for a worldwide Communist insurgency. Far from peaceful, this vision in fact bordered on genocidal. After the Cuban missile crisis, he told the *London Daily Worker*, "If the missiles had remained, we would have used them against the very heart of the U.S., including New York. We must never establish peaceful coexistence. In this struggle to the death between two systems, we must gain the ultimate victory. We must walk the path of atomic liberation even if it costs millions of atomic victims."[33]

This is the true face of today's ultimate leftist icon: that of a psychopath.

exposing their positions. American bombs were also better designed, weighed far less, and delivered a greater nuclear payload.[31]

The bottom line was that American military technology dominated that of the Soviets, notwithstanding Kennedy's false campaign warnings of a "missile gap." America's position was further strengthened because the Cuban missile crisis took place at sea, close to U.S. shores, which disadvantaged Russia's undersized navy.

The Cuban Missile Crisis was Kennedy's finest hour. Soviet leaders who thought they were dealing with a weak, inexperienced playboy realized they had entered into a contest of wills they could not win. Kennedy publicly declared that he did not seek war, but he made it clear that he would not stand for the missiles' installation in Cuba. The crisis began to subside when Kennedy astutely responded to a somewhat conciliatory letter from Khrushchev, ignoring a belligerent follow-up that the Soviet premier was pushed to send by other Politburo members. Eventually, the Soviets agreed to dismantle the missiles in exchange for American pledges not to invade Cuba and to remove U.S. missiles from Turkey at a later date. The batteries in Turkey were obsolete anyway, made redundant by the enhanced capabilities of new American nuclear subs.

Castro's reaction to the crisis was telling. Using the Brazilian government as an intermediary, the United States put out feelers during the missile crisis for a rapprochement, indicating to Castro that the two nations could have warm relations if Cuba would give up the missiles and stop trying to export Communist revolution. But Castro would not be mollified.[34] Even as United States and Soviet leaders were hammering out an agreement, on October 27, 1962, Castro wired Khrushchev asking the Soviet leader to launch a "pre-emptive" nuclear attack on the United States.[35] Realizing this would lead to a nuclear holocaust and decimate much of the Earth's population, the Soviet premier demurred.

Kennedy's tax cuts and the roller-coaster 1960s economy

In domestic policy, Kennedy's signature economic achievement actually occurred after his death. Although he is revered by liberals today, Kennedy was an emphatic proponent of tax cuts. His program for wide and deep tax relief was finally approved by his successor, President Johnson—though it didn't last long.

Before the 1960s, the U.S. economy was hamstrung by high income tax rates. These dated back to the presidency of Herbert Hoover, when the maximum federal income tax rate was lifted from 25 percent to 63 percent. Predictably, the tax hike choked economic activity, killed jobs, and served as one of the main, if less-mentioned, causes of the Great Depression. More than a decade later, to pay for the immense cost of fighting World War II, the government raised the top income tax rate even further, eventually hitting an amazing 92 percent.

The United States emerged from the war as the world's dominant economy, partly due to the simple fact that most of our major trading rivals had been damaged or even leveled in the fighting. The economy grew robustly in the Truman years, then slowed under President Eisenhower and underwent several recessions as continuing high tax rates took a toll on new business creation. Small business creation was particularly hampered, since there was little incentive for workers to go out on their own and try to create new companies. This gave rise to the perception of the 1950s as a decade dominated

Basic Economics in Action

"I was in that exceedingly high tax bracket after World War II, and I know what *I* did. I would be offered scripts for motion pictures, and, once I had reached that bracket, I just turned 'em down. I wasn't going to go to work for six cents on the dollar."

—**Ronald Reagan**[36]

by the "organization man"—an anonymous, conformist employee working for a big corporation.

This was the situation that confronted Kennedy when he ran for president in 1960. The intellectual underpinnings of his economic views—supply-side economic theory and the Laffer Curve—did not yet exist, yet Kennedy realized that high taxes were hurting the economy. So during his campaign he talked up a massive cut in income tax rates and capital gains tax rates, including a vow to lop the maximum income tax rate from 92 percent to 70 percent.

Although Kennedy failed to get his tax cuts approved in Congress, after his death Johnson took up the mantle and pushed the measure through. The effect was exhilarating. Unemployment fell from 5.4 percent in 1964 to 4.0 percent just two years later. The new economic activity boosted federal revenue from $86.9 billion in 1964 to $106.5 billion in 1967, with GNP soaring from $620.5 billion to $755 billion.[37]

Wall Street: Let the Good Times Roll

The stock market of the early and mid-1960s has become known as the "go-go market." Not only did prices rally, but the number of investors expanded from 8.1 million in 1956 to 20.1 million in 1965. This coincided with a boom in initial public offerings of major technology companies like Polaroid and Packard Instruments, the forerunner of Hewlett-Packard. The shares of these new securities often jumped 25 percent and even 50 percent on the first day of trading. The Wall Street boom led to new innovations in finance, notably the advent of credit cards, with Visa appearing in 1963 followed by Mastercard in 1965.[39]

Unfortunately, the economic boom Johnson unleashed in the mid-1960s was eventually undermined by Johnson himself. Concerned about inflation, the President's Council on Economic Advisors issued a report on December 26, 1965, calling for a massive tax increase to prevent the economy from overheating. The council's head, H. Gardner Ackley, even gave a speech warning of the "problem" of excessively high corporate profits.[38]

Fatefully, Johnson heeded his advisors' counsel. In March 1966, he gave a speech to 150 leading business executives asking their support for higher taxes. Not one corporate leader obliged.[40] Equally negative was the reaction of union leaders to Johnson's proposed "surcharges" of 7.5 percent on incomes, estates, and trusts, 10 percent on corporations, and 5 percent on capital gains, along with new excise taxes on cars.[41] It took Johnson some time to overcome popular opposition, but helped by huge Democratic majorities in the House and Senate, he eventually got the tax hikes passed in June 1968, only to be followed by proposed continuations and further increases.[42] The stock market, which was enjoying bullish growth going into 1966, stalled out right around the time Johnson began advocating the tax hikes, failing to regain its peak for the rest of the decade.[43] Johnson had betrayed Kennedy's tax-cutting credo, and the market went into an extended slump—aside, that is, from a spiteful 4 percent spike following Johnson's March 1968 announcement that he would not run for re-election.[44]

A final nail in the coffin of 1960s prosperity came at the end of the decade, at the hands of a Nixon appointee. Richard Nixon is often regarded as a conservative counterpoint to the Democratic presidencies that preceded him. But while Nixon may have capably defended the theory of free enterprise in his kitchen debate with Khrushchev, once he became president in 1969 he made a decision that had devastating economic effects—he appointed John Mitchell as attorney general.

Mitchell had made his name on Wall Street at the firm of Nixon, Mudge, Rose, Guthrie & Alexander, where he became known for devising a dubious legal instrument called the "moral obligation" bond. Here's how Mitchell's crafty little novelty works: states and municipalities rely on bond issues to pay for large-scale capital projects. To prevent irresponsible spending, they are required by their state constitutions or municipal charters to get the approval of voters for these bond issues. But, as we know, politicians are always looking to spend more money in order to entice campaign contributions from the individuals, contractors, developers, and unions that benefit from their spending. So Mitchell devised an end-run around requirements that voters be consulted on bond issues. Working for New York governor Nelson Rockefeller in 1960, he wrote a legal opinion supporting what is now called a "moral obligation bond," which ultimately allowed New York's Housing Finance Authority to sell unauthorized securities.[45] These bonds note that they are *not* backed by the state's constitution or approved by voters, but that the state has a "moral obligation" to honor it anyway. Mitchell then became a leading counselor to other states and cities eager to use this device, earning millions in advisory fees. Backed by liberal jurists, this legal sophistry has been used by politicians in nearly every state over the last four decades as a means to ignore voters' express guidance and to saddle the taxpayers with expensive debt.

Later, as attorney general, Mitchell inexplicably decided to strangle Wall Street, where he'd made his own fortune. Granted, at the time there was some popular dissatisfaction with corporate America. First, as stock ownership rapidly expanded throughout the 1960s, some individual investors were wiped out through no fault of their own when their brokerages went bankrupt. (The Security Investor Protection Corporation, which protects individual accounts, wasn't created until 1973.) Second, a select number of people who made fortunes in stocks sparked widespread jealousy and resentment. A prime example here was stock analyst Gerald Tsai Jr., who became famous in the 1960s after getting rich by trading in obscure but fast-rising technology stocks for his Fidelity Capital Fund.[46] And finally, some people were unsettled by the rise of the conglomerate in the 1960s, when "diversification" became the rage of corporate CEOs, leading to the creation of large, complex companies such as Gulf & Western, Litton Industries, ITT, and LTV. Their stocks reached wild heights that defied traditional measures of stock valuation, making them targets of populist anger.

A Book You're Not Supposed to Read

The Way the World Works by Jude Wanniski (Lanham, MD: Lexington Books, 1989).

Seeking to harness this resentment, Mitchell insisted that the growth of these companies—which were not dominant in any field—was dangerous to the average Joe and had to be stopped. It was not the government which was too powerful, but the corporate chieftains, he declared. Consequently, Mitchell's Justice Department filed lawsuits to prevent LTV's bid for a steel company, Litton's attempted purchase of a German typewriter company, an attempted sale of the B. F. Goodrich tire company, and many other harmless corporate transactions.[47] This further dampened the stock market by putting an effective cap on share prices and making mergers and acquisitions—then a burgeoning business—far more difficult.

Ironically, after Mitchell moved over to guiding Nixon's re-election, he arranged for secret campaign contributions to stop anti-trust actions against ITT, and he cozied up to financier Robert Vesco, who had stolen $500 million from the Investors Overseas Services fund in the largest fraud of the 1970s.[48] Vesco then fled to Cuba, where he lived lavishly for decades with Castro's connivance. In America, meanwhile, the last vestiges of Kennedy's pro-business, tax-cutting policies were wiped out until the ascendency of Ronald Reagan a decade later.

Sickness in secret

In light of Kennedy's passionate anti-communism, he is a curious focus for liberal myth-making. Much of this revolves around Kennedy's youthful charisma. But the enduring legend of Camelot obscures the truth about Kennedy's physical condition; in fact, his health was so poor that he was given the last rites at least four times.[49]

While Kennedy was young and handsome, his aides deceived the public about his shocking sickliness. One of his primary ailments was a debilitating back problem that was so serious he had surgery in 1944 when he just twenty-seven, and again in 1954 and 1955. Because of his back condition, at various times he couldn't put on his own shoes, had to be lifted by aides into his car, had to walk sideways down stairs, and was forced to use crutches. His Secret Service agents discussed the likelihood that if Kennedy were elected to a second term he would serve it in a wheelchair.[50]

Kennedy suffered throughout his life from a string of other disorders including scarlet fever, whooping cough, a severe bowel disorder, German measles, and yellow jaundice, the latter forcing his departure from Princeton. He was also repeatedly given sulfa drugs, most likely to treat sexually transmitted diseases, and he may have contracted malaria during his naval service in World War II.[51]

Furthermore, he received his first diagnosis for Addison's disease in 1947, before his election to the Senate. Because he had blatantly lied to reporters about it, Kennedy kept this diagnosis secret throughout his whole life.[52] The falsification continued after his death; in his book *The Thousand Days*, historian and Kennedy aide Arthur Schlesinger Jr. failed to mention it.[53] The disease forced Kennedy to take daily steroid injections that in turn gave him chronic urinary, skin, and respiratory infections requiring constant antibiotic treatments. Ejaculation and urination were painful, sometimes excruciating.[54]

As a result of these ailments, President Kennedy was constantly drugged up by painkillers, amphetamines, and other medications. According to a recent physician's review of his medical records,

> By the time he was president, he was on ten, 12 medications a day. He was on antispasmodics for his bowel, paregoric, lamodal transatine [ph], he was on muscle relaxants, Phenobarbital, Librium, Meprobomate, he was on pain medications, Codeine, Demerol, Methadone, he was on oral cortisone; he was on injected cortisone, he was on testosterone, he was on Nembutal for sleep. And on top of that he was getting injected sometimes six times a day, six places on his back, by the White House physician, with Novocain, Procaine, just to enable him to face the day.[55]

Whether the testosterone injections induced so-called "Roid Rage" or the amphetamine shots prompted depression is unclear. But Kennedy was certainly capable of moodiness, coldness, and sadism. Indeed, by most accounts these were primary motifs of his sexuality.

This brings up the most embarrassing aspect of "Camelot"—that John Kennedy had Secret Service agents bring hookers into the White House. In light of the testimony of numerous agents who spoke after Jackie Kennedy's death, this is no longer in dispute; Kennedy was supplied with prostitutes, some regularly joining him for naked swims in the White House pool.[56] Marilyn Monroe's famous sultry singing of "Happy Birthday" at Kennedy's 1962 birthday party in Madison Square Garden looks pretty shameless once you know that she was one of Kennedy's mistresses.[57]

⚛ ☮ ⚛ ☮ ⚛ ☮ ⚛ ☮ ⚛ ☮ ⚛ ☮ ⚛ ☮ ⚛

JFK: The Lunatic Fringe Comes to Hollywood

Kennedy's assassination in Dallas on November 22, 1963, gave rise to legions of outlandish conspiracy theories. One leftwing fringe theory is that dozens of rogue CIA agents joined businessman Clay Shaw and many others in a vast conspiracy to kill Kennedy to prevent him from pulling U.S. troops out of Vietnam—an action that Kennedy, in fact, had never planned. This preposterous notion received a new lease on life in 1991 with the release of *JFK*, directed by Oliver Stone and starring Kevin Costner.

The film is rife with inanities, innuendo, and lies; one investigation found one hundred outright falsehoods.[58] In *JFK*, the conspiracy is pieced together by a handful of witnesses who are invested with a credibility they never had in real life. One of the witnesses, Charles Speisel, has claimed to be a victim of mass mind-control experiments conducted by the New York City police. He also revealed that he fingerprinted his daughter when she left home for college and again when she returned home to ensure the government had not switched her with an imposter.[59] Another witness, Vernon Bundy, was an imprisoned junkie who failed a polygraph test and later admitted to other inmates that he'd made up his story to get an early release.[60]

Perhaps most damning, Oliver Stone used *Crossfire* as one of his two main sources for the script. The book's author, Jim Marrs, also wrote *Alien Agenda*, a "study" of alien invaders who allegedly control the United States government.

Kennedy also shared a mistress, Judith Campbell Exner, with the head of the Chicago mafia, even though he was specifically told by his brother, the attorney general, not to see her, as she represented an obvious public relations and intelligence risk.

In addition, while there can be no denying Kennedy's wit and charm, claims of his intellectual brilliance are risible. Theodore Sorensen is but one of several men who wrote the books and speeches that carry Kennedy's name, including the Pulitzer Prize-winning *Profiles in Courage*.[61] In fact, Kennedy had such difficulty distinguishing between fiscal and monetary policy that he relied on aides and memory tricks to explain the different roles played by the Federal Reserve and the Treasury Department.[62]

Kennedy's assassination, however, instantly turned the late president into a martyr—so much so that his entire extended family gained the status of American nobility. His presidency was mythologized as "Camelot," a reference to a popular musical that ran on Broadway from December 1960 to January 1963. This was meant to convey the image of a youthful, vigorous, happy, and dutiful president. *Camelot*, of course, is really about royalty and infidelity—much more fitting themes for the Kennedy presidency.

☮

Chapter Eleven

JOHNSON'S WAR ON POVERTY— AND COMMON SENSE

Through most of the 1960s, the number of poor Americans declined, continuing a trend from the previous decade. Then, around 1968, a strange thing happened: the number of Americans in poverty stopped dropping, even if one counts government benefits as income. Although the average household income has continued to rise in the four decades since, the poverty level has never fallen below the 1968 low of 13 percent, and rarely has it even dropped back down to that. In 1980, the poverty rate was 22 percent—almost 70 percent higher than twelve years earlier.[1]

Now this might seem strange, since President Johnson in January 1964 declared a "War on Poverty," which would become the centerpiece of his "Great Society" program. Poverty rates were already falling then, coinciding with the economic boom of the early-to-mid 1960s, but by the time Johnson relinquished the presidency five years later, poverty rates were rebounding strongly. What's more, the War on Poverty quickly ushered in dramatic increases in a wide range of social pathologies—crime, illegitimacy, drug abuse, and welfare dependency, to name a few. A generation of young, urban minorities began acting in harmful ways that had not been predicted by the statisticians and sociologists whose work had justified the War on Poverty programs.

Guess What?

⚛ The "War on Poverty" harmed the poor

⚛ The Great Society was marked by soaring crime and increasing drug abuse

⚛ The United States today spends more on welfare entitlements than it does on the military

Why? It's hard to prove that any pattern of human behavior is caused by one thing. People are complicated, after all, and our actions usually have many causes, the sources of which may be hard to unravel. But if any modern socioeconomic trend can be tied to a specific set of government policies, it's the breakdown of the American inner cities and the commencement of Johnson's "War on Poverty."

The War on Poverty entailed a massive increase in federal welfare spending. These programs grew and grew, attracting more and more recipients at greater and greater expense. Food stamps, for example,

Is That All?

Among other welfare schemes, the War on Poverty created or greatly expanded the following federal programs:

- food stamps
- job training courses
- community development block grants
- urban redevelopment and regional development schemes
- Medicaid
- Aid to Families with Dependent Children
- Social Security disability income
- Section 8 housing grants
- emergency assistance to needy families with children
- college scholarship aid
- free and reduced price school lunches
- child care programs
- construction of housing projects
- Head Start

began in 1965 with 424,000 recipients. By 1971, this had increased ten-fold to 4.4 million, and by 1980 it had reached 21.1 million—a growth of nearly fifty times in less than a generation.[2] Similarly, as Social Security disability standards were loosened, the number enrolled in that program grew from 687,000 in 1960 to 4,352,000 in 1975—a rise of 533 percent.[3] Federal job training included more than 32 million people by 1980, while total federal anti-poverty spending increased by twenty times between 1950 and 1980 in constant dollars.[4]

Especially targeted at poor blacks, the War on Poverty had widespread effects in the inner city—nearly all of them negative, and often downright destructive. One of the most dramatic effects was that enormous numbers of young black males left the regular labor force, with unemployment rates of young black males skyrocketing in comparison to those of young white males.[5]

Liberal explanations for this trend have all fallen flat. While some of this change stemmed from a decline in the quantity of agricultural work available to black sharecroppers in the rural South, this only explains a fraction of the shift. Racism also fails to explain the trend; most tellingly, it was only young blacks who were exiting the work force, with unemployment rates of black males over the age of 35 actually *falling* 30 percent during the 1960s. In fact, wages of educated blacks rose even faster than the wages of educated whites.

The real reason for the exodus of young blacks from the labor force was that suddenly many of them didn't have to work anymore—in fact, the way welfare worked, the government was paying them *not* to work. What's more, with this kind of perverse incentive to stay unemployed, education was devalued. More and more young black men dropped out of school, making it nearly impossible for them to acquire the skills necessary for upward mobility. As it turned out, federal job programs, costly though these were, were hardly an answer. One study of the Manpower

Development and Training Act found that the program only boosted the wages of its participants by an average of $200 per year.[6]

Welfare programs were already creating social problems before the onset of the War on Poverty. The best example is Aid to Families with Dependent Children (AFDC), which began in the 1930s to assist families headed by widows. Over time, however, the program started to pay for increasing numbers of families headed by divorced and never-married women. Since more children for such women meant more AFDC aid, poor women were effectively encouraged to have more babies—and to have them out of wedlock, since marriage usually meant an end to their benefits.

The Johnson administration greatly expanded this already dysfunctional program, creating a nightmare in America's inner cities. The AFDC caseload expanded 107 percent in the 1960s, with 71 percent of this increase taking place after the 1964 announcement of the War on Poverty. The growth in caseloads was especially rapid in the five largest United States cities, which saw a stunning 217 percent rise during the decade.[7] Almost overnight New York found that it had more than one million people on the dole—nearly one in four New Yorkers of working age.[8] The costly AFDC benefits were supplemented even further by new programs like food stamps.

A Book You're Not Supposed to Read

Losing Ground: American Social Policy, 1950-1980 by Charles Murray (New York: Basic Books, 1995).

Attempts to improve the welfare system backfired badly. The government began allowing welfare recipients to work part-time, but this simply increased the overall amount of money a woman could collect by staying on AFDC and avoiding marriage. The Johnson administration issued rules stopping case workers from visiting AFDC beneficiaries, for the government no longer was in a position to prevent boyfriends exploiting their girlfriends' aid payments. Tolerance for this kind of exploitative cohabitation was eventually mandated by the Warren Court in *King v. Smith* (1968).

In just a few years, the War on Poverty changed the economic calculus of life in the inner-city. Women were given a financial incentive to stay single, have babies, and avoid full-time work; and young men were give a financial incentive to get their girlfriends pregnant, not marry them, and live off the AFDC payments, rather than find work. These ill effects were magnified by government Section 8 housing grants for unwed mothers, which effectively gave teenage girls the option of getting pregnant, leaving their parents' home, and having the government pay for their apartment. Sociologist Charles Murray showed that in Pennsylvania in certain years the combination of welfare and part-time work provided twice as much income to a young couple as did marriage and regular low-wage employment, even when one did not include the value of federal housing aid available to welfare recipients.[9]

The most pernicious effect of the War on Poverty was that it destroyed the black family. During the key years of anti-poverty spending, the black illegitimacy rate more than doubled, going from 23 percent in 1963 to 48 percent in 1980.[10] And it has been impossible to re-establish marriage as a norm since, with black illegitimacy today approaching a catastrophic rate of 70 percent. Stable families are the best preventer of a wide variety of social ills—from crime to poverty. The welfare system destroyed that for people in the inner city, who were pimped into welfare dependence.

A host of pathologies infected the inner city once marriage and steady work were devalued. Without family or job responsibilities, young black men were much more prone to petty crime—and not-so-petty crime. After falling 22 percent from 1950 to 1960, homicide rates climbed 122 percent between 1963 and 1980.[11] Blacks were also the main victims of this crime wave, with black victimization rates rising 109 percent for rape and 372 percent for robbery between 1965 and 1979.[12] By 1966, blacks were seven times more likely to be victims of a robbery than were middle-class whites. Police responded by arresting masses of young black men; the arrest rate of blacks for violent crime shot up 866 percent between 1966 and 1970.[13] But with fewer convictions and shorter sentences due to Warren Court rulings, criminals were allowed to rule many inner city neighborhoods, preying on the majority of law-abiding citizens.[14]

What common sense and experience has told us—that welfare dependency destroys the family and erodes the work ethic—was confirmed in a series of controlled experiments in the 1970s in which sociologists gave poor young couples money whether or not they worked. The couples understood that the experiment would end after a few years, at which time they'd probably need job experience to present to prospective employers. In repeated studies in cities nationwide, the subjects worked less when they were receiving the payments. Most important, the payments served to break up black families; a New Jersey study found black couples who received the payment were 66 percent more likely to split up.[15]

Lyndon Johnson's motivations for the War on Poverty are subject to debate. Some view the program as an attempt to win new votes for the Democrats. This it most certainly did, creating a huge new welfare constituency that was dependent on the Democrats to keep their payments coming. Others believe Johnson was a liberal true believer, simply unable to see the self-defeating nature of his policies. Either way, Johnson promised America a "Great Society," but ended up delivering something else—a welfare state.

Just saying "yes"

Along with rising rates of crime, unemployment, and family breakdown in the inner cities came a new epidemic of drug abuse, particularly heroin. In 1967 the federal government estimated there were

60,000–200,000 heroin addicts in the United States, with the number rising to between 500,000 and one million by the early 1990s.[16]

The fate of 1960s-era heroin addicts was horrifying. According to a long-term study of 581 young heroin addicts initiated by UCLA in 1966, three decades later "284 had died, 21.6 percent from drug overdoses or from poisonings by adulterants added to the drug. Another 38.6 percent died from cancer or from heart or liver disease. Three died of AIDS. Homicides, suicides or accidents killed 55 of them." Nor were the survivors living happy lives. Varying from their late forties to their mid-sixties in age, more than two-fifths were still using heroin while others had switched to other drugs or alcohol. Many of those still living had serious health problems like chronic liver disease or HIV.[17]

A Hero Fit for Hollywood

One particularly despicable heroin smuggler, Frank Lucas, bragged of hiding the drug in the coffins of U.S. soldiers. In a typical example of Hollywood's inverted morality, his crimes are glamorized in the movie *American Gangster*, starring Denzel Washington.

The harmful consequences of spreading drug abuse in the inner cities went beyond the addicts themselves. The violence and territoriality associated with drug dealing became a permanent fact of life for inner city residents, even as the drug of choice changed over time from heroin to various forms of cocaine. Public housing projects came to be dominated by violent, drug dealing predators, and drug abuse played a prominent role in the rise of the culture of sexual promiscuity that led to the explosion of sexually transmitted diseases.[18]

Aside from inner city residents, drug use spread among another class of Americans during the 1960s. As mentioned in chapter 5, psychedelic drugs, including mescaline and especially LSD, became widespread within the counterculture. These drugs even found a following among self-styled intellectuals, who were especially influenced by Aldous Huxley's *The Doors of Perception*, the book from which the 1960s band The Doors took their name. Because there is little if any chance of overdosing on LSD, many users were unaware of its risks, especially its capacity to induce crippling depression and suicidal thoughts. A further danger stems from LSD's tendency to eat away at a person's ego and sense of self, a characteristic that made it useful to cult leaders like Charles Manson, who encouraged his devotees to indulge in the drug.

Legal Abortion: Another Legacy of the 1960s

At the same time the black community was being victimized by increasing crime and drug abuse rates, it faced another, less-noticed epidemic. Although abortion was legalized nationwide by the *Roe v. Wade* decision in 1973, restrictions on the procedure actually began loosening in many states in the 1960s. Before *Roe v. Wade*, sixteen states had liberalized their abortion laws, often so that a woman could get an abortion merely by getting a doctor to sign a note saying it would serve her mental health. Colorado was the first state to permit abortion under broad perimeters in 1967, and by 1970 the country's two largest states, New York and California, had followed. In New York, abortions were permitted up to the twenty-fourth week of pregnancy.

Since 1973, black women have been twice as likely as white women to have an abortion, denying an estimated 15 million black babies their right to life.[19] While Jesse Jackson is not prone to penetrating social insights, perhaps he had one in the 1970s, when he denounced abortion as "genocide" against the black community. It was a "genocide" he had apparently learned to live with, however, so he has since become an abortion supporter.

The great cost of the Great Society

The failures of the Great Society came at a high financial price.

Fifteen years ago, Rush Limbaugh pointed out, "Between 1965 and 1994, welfare spending has cost the taxpayers $5.4 trillion in constant 1993 dollars. The War on Poverty has cost us 70 percent more than the total price tag for defeating both Germany and Japan in World War II, after adjusting for inflation."[20] And the cost has only risen since.

Originally presented as a low-cost public benefit program for the indigent, Medicaid now costs $276.4 billion per year, with its accumulated costs accounting for around half the total U.S. debt. The expense of Great Society entitlement programs far exceeds all military spending even when, as currently, the country is at war in multiple theaters.

The enormous cost and scope of the Great Society could only have been conceived by a megalomaniac. Known in Texas as an "FDR man," Lyndon Johnson had grandiose pretensions to introduce a larger version of the New Deal, cost and consequence be damned. The speechwriter who prepared the address in which Johnson called for his "Great Society" had referred to a "good society." But that wasn't grand enough for Johnson, so he changed the phrasing.[21] Here is what Johnson said in that speech, addressed to a group of college students:

> I intend to establish working groups to prepare a series of White House conferences and meetings—on the cities, on natural beauty, on the quality of education, and on other emerging challenges. And from these meetings and from this inspiration and from these studies we will begin to set our course toward the Great Society.
>
> ...For better or for worse, your generation has been appointed by history to deal with those problems and to lead America toward a new age. You have the chance never before afforded to any people in any age. You can help build a society

where the demands of morality, and the needs of the spirit, can
be realized in the life of the Nation.

...Will you join in the battle to build the Great Society, to
prove that our material progress is only the foundation on
which we will build a richer life of mind and spirit?

There are those timid souls who say this battle cannot be
won; that we are condemned to a soulless wealth. I do not
agree. We have the power to shape the civilization that we
want.

But the government, in fact, did not have the power to create a new and
better society simply because it was willing to spend money profusely.
One of the best examples is education. Johnson persuaded Congress to set
up the federal Department of Education, even though the Constitution
does not give the federal government authority over education, which
was traditionally a matter for the states. The result was a travesty: test
scores peaked in 1964, the very year that the department was established,
and have never been as high since. As federal spending increased,
schools only worsened. With federal involvement came increased
bureaucracy and new federal demands, even as teachers became less and
less accountable thanks to unionization rules that presidents Kennedy
and Johnson had approved. Meanwhile, court rulings stripped teachers
of much of their classroom authority, rendering some classrooms all but
uncontrollable.

The Great Society produced one failing program after another, all conceived in the blind belief that the government can solve any problem if it
just throws enough money at it. To improve the cities, Johnson proposed
to "re-build the entire urban United States." What really resulted was the
construction of vast numbers of cheap housing projects—ugly, dangerous
places where no one wanted to live. Johnson's administration also set up
the National Endowment for the Arts. While we have yet to see any

modern-day Michelangelos or Beethovens emerge from NEA programs, the endowment became famous for funding the creation or exhibition of "artworks" like Andre Serrano's "Piss Christ," a photograph of a crucifix posed in the photographer's urine, and pornographic photographs of Robert Mapplethorpe inserting a bullwhip into his anus.

Johnson's megalomania may have been partly motivated by his poor health. He had serious heart trouble before he became president and died from a heart attack just four years after leaving office. Like the ancient pharaohs, he wanted to leave a giant monument to himself that would last through the ages. In the end, although he did not eliminate poverty or create a new, great society, he did secure a legacy—a bigger government that fails on a bigger scale.

Chapter Twelve

THE VIETNAM WAR: SNATCHING DEFEAT FROM THE JAWS OF VICTORY

During the 1960s, North Vietnamese Communist leader Ho Chi Minh became a folk hero among much of the New Left. Radicals marched through America's streets chanting Ho's name and urging his Communist forces on to victory. Only Castro, Che, and Mao rivaled Ho's popularity.

The radicals' adoration of "Uncle Ho" was shared by many liberal journalists. Just as *New York Times* reporter Herbert Matthews gushed over Castro, so the *Times*'s most respected foreign correspondent, Harrison Salisbury, labored on behalf of Ho, ignoring even the pretense of objectivity. In fact, while the United States was still at war against Ho's forces, Salisbury authored an introduction to a collection of Ho's diaries. Praising Ho as a "poet-philosopher" with "the soul of a dragon," Salisbury's effusive preface depicts Ho as a modern-day philosopher-king.[1]

The veneration of Ho also infected our intellectual class. America's two most influential Asia scholars of the twentieth century, Harvard University's John King Fairbank and Edwin Reischauer, both argued Ho had no connection to international Communism.[2] This insistence was echoed by acclaimed journalist and author David Halberstam, who argued that one needed to "perceive nuances. . . . Ho, although a Communist, might also be primarily Vietnamese and under no orders from Moscow."[3]

Guess What?

- Although the Left denies it, Ho Chi Minh was a lifelong Communist

- The Viet Cong were demoralized and defeated before the United States left Vietnam

- The media transformed the 1968 Tet Offensive from an overwhelming American victory into a devastating defeat

175

This became a standard refrain of the Left: Ho was much more a nationalist than a Communist. And if he allied himself with Communists, it was only because America had spurned him. It was the same argument they initially made about Castro: somehow, it must be America's fault.

Communist Modesty

Ho Chi Minh's carefully cultivated image as a modest ascetic was largely bunk. Born Nguyen Ai Quoc, his adopted name was an arrogant *nom de guerre* that meant "Ho, the Enlightened One." He also had a number of affairs with both Western and Vietnamese women, secretly married twice, and was most likely a bigamist.[4]

Ho's own history leaves no doubt that he was a committed Communist. He lived in London in his youth and later moved to France, where he said he underwent the most important event of his political education: the reading of Lenin's "Theses on the National and Colonial Question."[5] As Ho put it, "By studying Marxism-Leninism in parallel with political participation, I gradually came upon the fact that only Socialism and Communism can liberate the oppressed nations and the working people throughout the world." He added,

Finally I was able to grasp the essential part. What emotion, enthusiasm, enlightenment and confidence they communicated to me! I wept for joy. Sitting by myself in my room, I would shout as if I were addressing large crowds: "Dear martyr compatriots! This is what we need, this is our path to liberation!" Since then, I had entire confidence in Lenin.[6]

Ho went to work as a Communist activist, speaking and writing articles in support of world Communism, and joining the French Communist Party in 1921.[7] In June 1923 he went to Moscow for additional training. Ho cultivated wide-ranging Soviet connections, becoming personally acquainted with top Bolsheviks such as Zinoviev, Bukharin, and even Stalin himself.[8] He condemned the French socialists for their ostensible lack of radicalism, not even sparing the Soviets from similar criticism.[9] Profiled in Communist magazines, Ho also received advanced training in Marxism-Leninism at the Stalin School.[10]

Ho spent the next two decades as a Communist guerrilla organizer in China on behalf of the Comintern, the Soviet-led headquarters of international Communism. He established an armed force, the Indochinese Communist Party (constituted at various times as the Vietnamese Communist Party and the Viet Minh) with the goal of spreading Communism to Vietnam as well as to Cambodia, Thailand, and Laos.[11] Aided by Soviet support and Comintern funding, Ho's army by 1930 had taken control of a northern Vietnamese province from French forces. There Ho's followers committed mass murder against landlords and other ideological enemies while implementing a Soviet-style collectivization campaign.[12] The abolition of rural private property through collectivization—a bloody hallmark of Communist revolutions first attempted by Lenin during the Russian Civil War—was land reform enforced by executions. It would be implemented by Ho more fully in the mid-1950s, when the estimated death toll reached between 100,000 and several hundred thousand.[13]

Ho's initial revolt ended ignominiously after French troops re-took the province, killing 2,000 of Ho's men and capturing 50,000 more.[15] Ho fled to Moscow, studied at the Lenin School, and then taught for several years at the Stalin School, supporting Stalin's government as the most murderous waves of the purges were taking place. He returned to Vietnam in 1938, reconstituting his forces with hundreds of war prisoners who had been released due to pressure from Communists in Leon Blum's Popular Front government in France.[16]

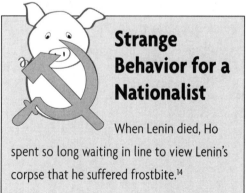

Strange Behavior for a Nationalist

When Lenin died, Ho spent so long waiting in line to view Lenin's corpse that he suffered frostbite.[14]

At the end of World War II, Ho Chi Minh's fighters took over most of Vietnam's major cities. Ho declared himself the country's provisional president and presided over a gruesome campaign of mass murder as the Communists sought to wipe out their nationalist rivals, even though Ho had pledged to work with them. Ho's chief opponent was the Nationalist Party led by Ngo Dinh Diem, a former colonial administrator turned independence fighter. Diem survived repeated Communist assassination attempts and at one point hid in a monastery in New Jersey.[17] Others were not so lucky—the Communists shot Nationalist Party leaders Nguyen The Nghiep and Nguyen Ngoc Son, and they buried Diem's brother and closest companion, Ngo Dinh Khoi, alive. Ho's forces also killed the leaders of the Constitution Party, the Front of National Union, and the Da Viet Party,[18] murdering up to 50,000 nationalists by the end of 1946.[19]

The Communists murdered all kinds of perceived ideological enemies. They assassinated popular religious authorities like the prophetic leader of the Hoa Hao sect, Huynh Phu So, whose body was dismembered and the pieces hidden so that his followers couldn't bury and memorialize him.[21] The Viet Minh launched a campaign of murder against Huynh's devotees, displaying the corpses as an intimidation tactic.[22] Even Trotskyites were not spared in the carnage. Trotskyite leader Nguyen Ta Thu Thau was taken to a lonely stretch of beach and shot through the forehead.[23] Among other Trotskyite leaders, Phan Van Hum, Phan Van Chanh, and Tran Van Thach, were also slain.[24] Thousands of landowners, the great demons of Communist lore, were massacred as well.[25]

A Book You're Not Supposed to Read

The History of the Bolshevik Communist Party of the USSR by Joseph Stalin (New York: International Publishers, 1939; now available in the public domain, Marxists Internet Archive, 2008). This work was personally translated into Vietnamese by Ho Chi Minh.[20]

In denying Ho's lifelong Communism, the American Left simply regurgitated the propaganda devised by Ho himself, who routinely insisted to American or Western audiences that he was not really a Communist. When asked why, if he wasn't a Communist, he led the Vietnamese Communist Party, Ho simply asserted that he was a "revolutionary."[26] He even took to quoting from the Declaration of Independence, a simple propaganda tactic that liberals cite to this day as irrefutable proof that Ho was no Communist.

Lenin famously claimed Western supporters of Communism were "useful idiots." During the Vietnam War, the New Left seemed determine to prove him right.

Who were the real heroes in Vietnam?

Movies, TV shows, and books present a clear, consistent image of the two opposing sides in Vietnam: Americans are bumbling, callous, and reluctant soldiers; the Viet Cong and North Vietnamese fighters are fierce, highly motivated, and wily. None of this is true.

Let's begin with the birth of the Viet Cong, which the North Vietnamese Communists characterized as a spontaneous rebellion against the corruption and brutality of the American-backed South Vietnamese government. Popular with the American Left, this explanation was a main tenet of Stanley Karnow's Pulitzer Prize winning book, *Vietnam: A History*, which also served as the companion to a nationally televised documentary series on Public Television. What's strange about Karnow's claim is that Communist Vietnamese leaders had stopped making it by the time his book appeared in 1983. By then, General Giap and others had admitted what the most casual observer already knew: Ho's government had created the Viet Cong, tightly controlled them, and directed their military activities.[27] Much to the embarrassment of the American Left, after achieving victory, the Vietnamese Communists no longer needed to perpetuate their old myths. Instead, they wanted credit for all their work in organizing the entire war.

The image of Viet Cong soldiers as zealous, nearly invincible fighters was another lie. In fact, in every major battle the Viet Cong were cut down by American troops, whose kill ratios typically ranged between 25 to 1 and 40 to 1, reaching up to 158 to 1 in some units.[28] Even the U.S.-allied South Vietnamese troops (ARVN), often derided as incompetent, achieved lopsided kill ratios, with the best ARVN division, the 25th, hitting 25 to 1.[29] As one American lieutenant general observed about the Viet Cong, "They had plenty of modern weapons (AK-47s, etc.); however, they were not very good shots."[30]

Suffering such a high casualty rate, the Viet Cong were plagued by desertions. Over the course of the war, more than 200,000 former Communists defected, and many more Viet Cong simply deserted in hopes of returning to regular life.[31] Many Viet Cong had only enlisted in order to avoid horrific Communist reprisals, and after 1966 many if not most Viet Cong recruits were forcibly impressed into the guerilla army.[32] Due to casualties, defections, and reluctant recruits, by war's end the Viet Cong had been reduced to an almost trivial force: in 1973 only 25,000 Viet Cong remained in all of South Vietnam. The rest—numbering in the hundreds of thousands—had been wiped out, changed sides, or quit the fight.[33]

With the Viet Cong getting pulverized, the North Vietnamese Army (NVA) sent its own soldiers to reinforce them. In 1966, the North sent 69,000 soldiers south, with the number rising to more than 100,000 annually by 1969.[34] By that time more than two-thirds of the Communist forces in the South were Northerners.[35] And instead of the dedicated, highly motivated soldiers portrayed in the Western media, these were mostly grudging conscripts, some as young as thirteen.[36] Told that they'd be welcomed by South Vietnamese villagers who were supposedly living in dire poverty, NVA soldiers were often shocked and demoralized when they discovered they were widely disdained by Southerners, who actually enjoyed much higher living standards than the North.[37]

Insisting from the war's beginning that the Viet Cong were acting independently of Ho's government, many Western reporters had difficulty explaining the growing numbers of NVA soldiers fighting in the South. Some parroted North Vietnam's laughable explanation that these troops were volunteers acting on their own initiative. More typical, though, was the captured NVA soldier who told an interrogator he'd been "leading a peaceful life in the North where there was no war. Therefore, I did not want to go south where I was likely to get killed."[38]

The American media's false portrayal of the Communists as noble, highly motivated, fearsome fighters was only one part of its slanted war coverage. The other major mischaracterization was the portrayal of U.S. troops as vicious, inept, and unwilling fighters. In fact, as their officers and their battlefield results testified, Americans were not only brave and highly motivated, but highly effective, winning every major battle they fought, including those at Song Be, Dong Xoai, Con Thien, Khe Sanh, Hue, and Da Nang.

The rare instances of misconduct—from the killing of innocents at My Lai to, later in the war, incidents of severe indiscipline—were just that: rare. In fact, American soldiers not only fought the enemy but also waged a war for hearts and minds that mostly went unreported. The average American did not know that United States soldiers routinely aided Vietnamese villagers by stacking sandbags to combat seasonal flooding, provided metal sheets to help fortify their lean-tos and grass huts, dug wells, laid out roads, erected medical clinics, and rendered many other forms of aid.[39] And yet, while every American misdeed was reported, the media routinely downplayed or ignored Communist atrocities.

The media also showed no interest in covering the battlefield heroism of American troops. This was a sharp contrast from World War II, when

A Picture Is Worth a Thousand Lies

Perhaps the most famous image to emerge from the Vietnam War was the Pulitzer Prize winning photograph of South Vietnamese police chief Nguyen Ngoc Loan executing a man on the streets of Saigon. Although leftists cited the image as proof of the barbarism of America's South Vietnamese allies, the actual circumstances of the photo were hardly ever mentioned. As Loan revealed, the "victim" was the leader of a Viet Cong terrorist squad that had just murdered the entire family of one of Loan's deputies.[40]

One person who came to regret the picture was the photographer, Eddie Adams. Upon Loan's death in 1998, Adams wrote a eulogy bemoaning the one-sidedness of his famous photograph and hailing Loan as "a great warrior."[41]

newspapers avidly recorded the deeds of heroes like Medal of Honor winner Audie Murphy, who nearly single-handedly fought off a full squad of German soldiers. And despite the media's indifference, the Vietnam War produced plenty of American heroes. One such man was Private First Class Milton Lee Olive III, who threw himself on a grenade lobbed at his unit. The eighteen-year-old was killed, but his heroic act saved the lives of at least four of his fellow soldiers.

Another unsung hero was Medal of Honor winner Peter Lemon, who was serving on a base in Tay Ninh province in 1970 when it came under attack by 400 NVA regulars. Lemon led a crew of just eighteen Americans in holding off waves of attacks. During one assault, he carried a wounded comrade to safety under enemy fire, then took up a machine gun. Left completely exposed, he was wounded three times as he laid down a defensive line of fire. Finally out of bullets, with three friends dead beside him and every member of his platoon wounded, Lemon defended his position with just his bayonet. He later refused to evacuate from an aid station until all his wounded comrades were flown out.

But the image of brutal American soldiers better fit the media's narrative, so heroic stories were ignored. Returning to America, Vietnam veterans were denounced as "baby killers" and worse by leftists. And liberals in the media have continued their abuse of Vietnam veterans by routinely portraying them as embittered, broken men who are haunted by their service. This is one of the most heinous myths of all. In fact, 74 percent of veterans say they "enjoyed" their service in Vietnam, 71 percent are "glad" they went, and 66 percent report that they'd serve again.[42] Vietnam veterans are also better educated and earn higher salaries than their peers who did not serve.[43] And what really angers them? Eighty-two percent believe the "political leaders in Washington would not let them win."[44] American soldiers wanted victory, and they resented political orders that restrained their activities and limited their targets.

A defeated enemy is handed victory: The Tet Offensive

One turning point of the war was the 1968 Tet Offensive, a massive Communist assault on South Vietnam that included an attack on the United States Embassy. The offensive shocked American journalists, who flooded the media with reports that the war was unwinnable, the most famous coming from Walter Cronkite.

In their panicked state, however, reporters failed to notice an important detail: the Tet Offensive not only failed, it was a catastrophic defeat for the Communists, who are believed to have lost between 30,000 and 92,000 men, mostly from elite Viet Cong units.[45] The offensive was colossally mismanaged by its North Vietnamese organizers. Because of a change in the calendar that year, some Viet Cong units believed they were to strike on January 30, 1968, while others expected the assault to begin a day later. Thus, an attempted surprise attack on the American command headquarters south of Saigon completely failed because, among other reasons, half the attacking force showed up a day late. The Tet Offensive was so botched that some Viet Cong officers suspected North Vietnam had sabotaged the uprising in order to destroy the Viet Cong and place the entire war effort directly in the hands of NVA troops.[46]

Believing South Vietnam was about to crumble, North Vietnam had expected the offensive to provoke a popular uprising in the South, along with the large-scale defection of ARVN troops. Something closer to the opposite occurred: more and more South Vietnamese joined the ARVN as word spread of Communist atrocities committed during Tet. At the city of Hue, for example, the Viet Cong "rounded up many hundreds of civilians—known anti-Communists, students, Catholic priests, low-level government employees and their relatives. Perhaps as many as 2,800 of these were shot, bludgeoned to death, or buried alive."[47] In other places, the Viet Cong decapitated businessmen, landowners, and other supposed class enemies. As a Vietnamese peasant commented,

Before the Tet Offensive, 18-year old villagers would lie and say they were 13 to get out of the draft; after the Tet Offensive, 13- and 14-year olds would lie and say they were 18 to get into the draft before the Communists got to them. The perception of the craziness of what the Communists were doing was increased, and the idea that they were inevitable winners was so deflated that people changed very much how they felt.[48]

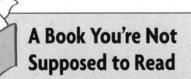

A Book You're Not Supposed to Read

Triumph Forsaken: The Vietnam War, 1954-1965 by Mark Moyar (Cambridge University Press, 2009)

Within eight months of Tet, ARVN desertion rates fell by nearly one-third, to around one per hundred.[49]

That is what really happened during and after Tet. But that is not what the media reported. Instead, the offensive was portrayed as a colossal defeat for the American military. Even though the Viet Cong were decimated, biased press coverage destroyed American confidence that we were winning the war—right at the moment of our biggest victory. In just nine months—from the fall of 1967 to the summer of 1968—the proportion of Americans who believed we were winning fell from a majority to one-fifth.[50]

Still, Americans didn't react as the media expected to the false reports that the war was lost. Instead of demanding withdrawal from Vietnam, they advocated a stronger military campaign. Less than two months after Tet began, antiwar candidate Eugene McCarthy received 42 percent of the vote in the New Hampshire Democratic primaries, provoking President Johnson to drop his bid for re-election. Subsequent polling, however, revealed that three-fifths of McCarthy's voters were casting protest ballots in favor of a *more aggressive* prosecution of the war.[51]

The media's skewed reports created an echo chamber in which reporters, Democratic Party politicians, and the "antiwar" movement constantly affirmed their common defeatist viewpoint, which became increasingly disconnected from the views of mainstream America. This was brought home in the 1972 election when Richard Nixon, who had taken command of the war from President Johnson and even expanded the war effort into Cambodia, trounced antiwar candidate George McGovern, beating him in 49 of 50 states. In the ultimate expression of life in the liberal echo chamber, *New Yorker* writer Pauline Kael proclaimed she was shocked by Nixon's victory: she didn't know one person who voted for him.

Why did the South lose?

Of course, America made mistakes in Vietnam, the most notable being the Kennedy administration's acquiescence to the 1963 coup by South Vietnamese generals against their president, Ngo Dinh Diem. Afterward South Vietnam suffered from poor leadership, which hurt the country's international reputation and the morale of its troops.

Even so, by the early 1970s the North's strategy of guerrilla warfare had unequivocally failed. The Viet Cong had suffered irreversible losses and their NVA replacements were having few successes against an increasingly hostile South Vietnamese population. According to one Communist official, by 1974 there were only 500 Communist cadres left in Saigon, a city of 2.5 million.[52] The following year, North Vietnamese premier Pham Van Dong admitted that up to 70 percent of Southerners opposed "reunification," and even this downplayed the true scale of opposition to Communist encroachments.[53] Things were also looking up for the Americans: the number of American troops in Vietnam fell from a peak of more than half a million to fewer than 70,000 in 1972, as they were replaced by ARVN soldiers through Nixon's "Vietnamization" strategy. Antiwar protest in America largely died out in 1973 after Nixon ended the draft, underscoring what really motivated the "antiwar" movement: selfishness and cowardice.

So how then did the North Vietnamese win? The same way that Hitler captured France and Poland: with tank battalions. Over the preceding generation, Communist governments had given North Vietnam an enormous amount of heavy artillery and other materiel for a large, mechanized standing army. China provided $670 million in military assistance before 1965 and approximately $2 billion over the following decade. The Soviet Union provided enormous help as well, including $705 million in aid in 1967 alone. More assistance poured in from other Warsaw Pact nations. This support took many forms: trucks, planes, grenades, rifles, artillery, ammunition, uniforms, oil, and engineers.[54]

This was not all. By 1973 NVA regulars in the South had 250 122- and 130-mm heavy guns, along with massed batteries of advanced surface to air missiles.[55] The Northern army ultimately captured Saigon with more than 600 T-54 Soviet tanks.[56] These were not guerilla weapons but those of large-scale armored infantry corps. Giving up the guerilla infiltration strategy in 1972, the NVA instead began sending divisions of regular mechanized army units to the South.

Even after introducing mechanized units, however, the NVA could not overcome the combination of ARVN ground troops and U.S. air power. The NVA's first big attack, the Easter Offensive of 1972, failed miserably under assault by bombing runs from American B-52s, with the Communists suffering more than 100,000 dead.[57] As a Communist general later put it, "Our troops were exhausted and their units in disarray. We had not been able to make up our losses. We were short of manpower as well as food and ammunition."[58] Later that year Nixon's "Christmas bombing" campaign dealt another devastating blow to the North. British counterinsurgency expert Sir Robert Thompson observed that at that point, America "had won the war. It was over! . . . [North Vietnam] would have taken any terms."[59]

But the South's fortunes spiraled downward as American aid was shut off by liberals in Congress. As Nixon's power waned with the Watergate scandal, the Democrats felt emboldened to act. Between 1973 and 1974, U.S. aid was cut by more than 55 percent; it fell nearly 30 percent the following year.[60] The consequences were soon felt in the field: ARVN battalions could not replace their artillery, soldiers received fewer bullets, and the few ARVN tanks ran short of gasoline. Supplies of bandages ran so low that medics began reusing them.[61]

When Congress ordered an end to American air support, South Vietnam's fate was

A Book You're Not Supposed to Read

Big Story by Peter Braestrup (New York: Presidio Press, 1994)

sealed. The North Vietnamese tied up ARVN ground troops and then launched a massive tank invasion. The whole NVA was now exposed to a possible air attack, but Democrats in Congress refused to allow U.S. bombers to strike. Saigon fell in 1975.

With Democrats outnumbering Republicans by more than 2 to 1, the Congress that abandoned South Vietnam was guided by a clique of antiwar activists who had struggled for years to undermine the war effort. One of their prominent leaders was Ronald Dellums. A self-proclaimed Socialist, Dellums is now a member of the Democratic Socialist Organizing Committee (DSOC), an offshoot of the Socialist Party of America, and he is former vice chairman of the Democratic Socialists of America.[62] Dellums began his tenure in Congress by holding hearings on American "war crimes." He was reluctant, though, to discuss Communist atrocities. This is unsurprising in light of his role models; in 1982 his congressional chief of staff sent a letter to Grenada's Marxist dictator, Maurice Bishop, identifying Bishop and Fidel Castro as the world leaders Dellums most admired.[63]

Another leader of Congress's antiwar faction was Bella Abzug, who had long been widely suspected of being a Communist; her Communist sympathies were detailed in a *New York Post* profile of her student activism in 1941. Abzug got a law degree, became active in the Communist-dominated National Lawyers' Guild, and is still regarded as a hero by the Trotskyite Spartacus League for her work defending Communist Party members.[64] Abzug also joined the leadership of two Communist front groups—the National Council of the Arts, Sciences, and Professions and the Civil Rights Congress. In 1971, on her first day in Congress, she introduced legislation demanding the withdrawal of all American troops from Vietnam. Abzug also warned against providing sanctuary to South Vietnamese opponents of Communism if the North should win, declaring our allies would deserve "the punishment that awaits them."[65]

In the end, Abzug got her wish. The Communist victory in South Vietnam produced horrific consequences: the country's conversion into a one-party state, massacres of non-Communist officials, the sentencing of hundreds of thousands to "re-education" camps, the suppression of religious expression, and the exodus of hundreds of thousands of boat people. What the South Vietnamese did to deserve such a fate is unclear, although in the eyes of Abzug and other radicals, their alliance with America was a cardinal sin.

Cambodian nightmare

Vietnamese Communism was bloody, but its outrages paled in comparison to the genocide that Communists unleashed on Vietnam's western neighbor. With the assistance of their Vietnamese comrades, the Cambodian Communists, the Khmer Rouge, launched an insurgency in 1968, finally seizing the Cambodian capital, Phnom Penh, in 1975. In converting the country to Communism, the Khmer Rouge undertook a shocking campaign of mass extermination against their own people resulting in an estimated 1.7 million deaths.

Unsurprisingly, Western liberals blamed the entire tragedy on America. This argument originated with British writer William Shawcross, who claimed the United States bombing of Cambodia during the Vietnam War—targeted at North Vietnamese supply lines along the Ho Chi Minh trail—provoked many Cambodians to support or join the Khmer Rouge, leading to their ultimate victory.

This argument overlooks the Khmer Rouge's *real* source of strength: the North Vietnamese Communists. Ho's forces had established camps, supply depots, and intelligence headquarters in Cambodia as early as 1962—long before America began bombing these sites.[67] The NVA also used Cambodia as a sanctuary from which they attacked American troops.[68]

In fact, the Vietnamese Communists were active in Cambodia even before that, and long before the Khmer Rouge were founded. As Pol Pot,

A Leftist Goes Too Far

One of the most determined opponents of American victory in Vietnam was MIT professor Noam Chomsky, who became a hero to the New Left for his denunciations of America's war effort and his downplaying and justifying of Communist brutality. Chomsky, however, managed to alienate even some committed leftists when he emerged as an apologist of the maniacal Khmer Rouge. Cavalierly dismissing the harrowing reports of Cambodian refugees as biased, Chomsky denied the Rouge had engaged in genocide, comparing their atrocities to scattered reprisals against collaborators in post-World War II France; the crimes were a small though regrettable price to pay for the good of the revolution, according to Chomsky. The professor later admitted that mass killings had occurred, but he continued to minimize their scale and deny they were ordered by the Khmer Rouge government, whose deranged policies he still defended.[66]

the Khmer Rouge's demented leader, commented, "There was no fighting in Cambodia" when he left the country for France in 1949.[69] Returning in 1953, he was surprised to find Viet Minh forces ambushing and killing people all over the country in a direct challenge to Cambodia's army and the country's king, Norodom Sihanouk.[70] When these actions sparked an anti-Communist crackdown, Cambodian Communists fled to a base in Krabao, Thailand, where they were tutored in Communist revolution by their Vietnamese brethren.[71] One of Pol Pot's aides would later admit, "The Vietnamese took all the decisions. We were just puppets."[72] Pol Pot and nearly 2,000 Cambodian Communists later moved from Krabao to Hanoi for further training.[73]

Over the next fifteen years, the Cambodian Communists alternated between a sporadic presence in Cambodia and exile in Vietnam, where they organized under the guidance of the Viet Cong and their North Vietnamese commanders. The Khmer Viet Minh, as they were sometimes called, set up new headquarters, known as Office 100, in the jungle a few miles from the Viet Cong headquarters in Ta Not, where they remained "under tight Viet Cong control."[74] A veteran of that camp would later note that the Cambodians had to "rely on the Vietnamese for everything, food, materials, security, the lot.... To go from one bureau to another we had to have a Vietnamese guard to escort us.... They were the hosts and we had to obey."[75]

After they gained power, the Khmer Rouge diverged from their Vietnamese tutors and were eventually deposed by them in the Vietnam-Cambodian War of 1975 to 1979. But before that break, it was Vietnam, not America, that supplied, sustained, and trained the Khmer Rouge. In fact, the Vietnamese even did a lot of the Cambodians' fighting for them. As author and former BBC correspondent Philip Short notes:

> Throughout 1970 and 1971, the brunt of the fighting in Cambodia was borne by the Vietnamese. The Khmer Rouge were a leavening, to make the Vietnamese units appear more acceptable to the population at large, or, if they fought separately, an auxiliary force, to occupy the territory once the Vietnamese had passed. It was not a Khmer Rouge unit that stormed the airport on the outskirts of Phnom Penh, but Vietnamese commandos from the elite Dac Cong brigade who, in a four-hour assault which left at least forty dead, blew up the whole of [Nationalist General] Lon Nol's air force—ten MiG-17's, five T-28 trainers, ten transport aircraft and eight helicopters—and two ammunition dumps. The same group later destroyed 60

percent of Cambodia's oil refinery storage in a raid on Kompong Som.[76]

This is an inconvenient truth for sixties leftists; with so many of them denying that Ho was even a Communist, how could they explain his role in nurturing the genocidal Cambodian Communists and guiding them to power? Well, the way they always do: blame it all on America.

Street theater: The 1968 Chicago riots

Perhaps the most famous protest against the Vietnam War was the rioting in Chicago outside the 1968 Democratic convention. The Democratic primaries that year were full of tension, accented by the assassination of a leading candidate, Robert Kennedy, by Palestinian nationalist Sirhan Sirhan. While the radicals favored antiwar stalwart Eugene McCarthy, as the convention approached they became increasingly incensed at the prospect of party bosses at the convention choosing a more mainstream candidate, Vice President Hubert Humphrey.

Lacking the numbers to stop Humphrey's nomination, the radicals decided to pressure the party from the streets. The protestors comprised various far-left groups with a penchant for violence, including the Black Panthers, Maoist organizations, the Yippies, and the "New York Motherfuckers," a gang described by a future Weather Underground member Susan Stern as "the dirtiest, skuzziest, and loudest group of people I ever laid eyes on."[77] The presence of motorcycle gang members heightened the threat of violence even further.

Students for a Democratic Society played a key organizing role. Although much of the media later described the riots as a spontaneous reaction to police brutality, a partici-

A Book You're Not Supposed to Read

Don't Tread on Me by Harry Crocker III (New York: Crown Forum, 2006)

pant in SDS preparations in Chicago testified to a carefully organized enterprise, reporting that the group had a "businesslike air about it; phones ringing constantly, 'sharp struggle' over tactics and other political issues; piles of leaflets and underground newspapers; and official-looking, serious people concerned with bail, medical care, housing, march permits, and legal aid, conferring constantly."[78]

The plan was simple—provoke the police. One of the more repugnant tactics was to send women to the front of protest marches. Chanting "Chicks Up Front," radicals did not make much of an effort to disguise this maneuver. Protestors further back, some wearing helmets in anticipation of violence, then pelted police with rocks, bricks, hunks of concrete, and water balloons filled with human waste.[79] When police moved to arrest the rioters they first had to wade through lines of women, creating media-ready agitprop worthy of the Bolsheviks.[80]

Seven of the riot's ringleaders, the so-called Chicago Seven, were prosecuted. (Black Panther leader Bobby Seale was tried separately.) The defendants retained top-flight legal talent including William Kunstler, a famous far-left lawyer who went on to defend Sheikh Omar Abdel-Rahman, the "Blind Sheikh" convicted of the 1993 World Trade Center bombing. Instead of fighting the charges, however, five of the defendants used the trial as a public opportunity to ridicule the legal process and hurl profanity at the judge.

The trial made heroes out of the defendants, who were hailed by radicals as innocent activists railroaded by a corrupt judicial system. But who were the Chicago Seven really? One defendant, Abbie Hoffman, was a bipolar cocaine dealer.[81] Giving the finger to the court officer who swore him in, Hoffman mocked the judge, the unrelated Julius Hoffman, calling him "a disgrace to the Jews" who "would have served Hitler better" and offering to introduce him to a dealer so the judge could buy LSD. After going on the lam for several years in the 1970s to avoid sentencing for a drug dealing charge, Abbie Hoffman committed suicide in 1989.

Another defendant was Tom Hayden, the former SDS president who during the Vietnam War made solidarity visits to Communist Cuba, Czechoslovakia, and North Vietnam. In Paris, Hayden advised Viet Cong leaders on psychological warfare techniques that would be effective against Americans. He also denounced as "propaganda" and "lies" the accurate reports that American prisoners of war were suffering torture in North Vietnam. When leftwing folk singer Joan Baez affirmed these reports, Hayden denounced her as a CIA tool.[82]

A third defendant, Rennie Davis, later became a follower of Indian cult leader Guru Maharaj Ji. Demonstrating his tenuous grip on reality, Davis extolled the Guru's 1973 speech at the Houston Astrodome as "the greatest event in history.... If we knew who he was we would crawl across America on our hands and knees to rest our heads at his feet."[83]

In a stark demonstration of the loss of self-confidence among American authorities, the Chicago Seven were allowed to turn their trial into a farce. And the outcome was no less absurd—the defendants were found not guilty of conspiracy, while convictions on other charges were overturned on the preposterous technicality that the judge had disallowed the defense from screening jurors about potential cultural bias. Another judge even refused to enforce the contempt citations issued against the defendants during the trial.

The Chicago Seven—like many "antiwar" radicals—presented themselves as brave souls resisting cruel authorities and a hypocritical capitalist order. The people who opposed them—the police specifically, and mainstream Americans in general—were denounced as corrupt squares threatened by the radicals' non-conformity and easy sexuality, and whose lives were driven by repression and a love of power.

History has shown, however, that it was the radicals who were power hungry. They fought for revolution, and not a libertarian one—their heroes were the Communists who had brought bloody, totalitarian dictatorships to Cuba, China, and elsewhere. Unable to gain power through democratic elections, they took to the streets to seize it for themselves.

Compare their actions to the Vietnam veterans they spat upon. Whether draftees or volunteers, veterans answered a call to duty and risked their lives to preserve the freedom of a distant people. Eschewing the narcissism and hedonism of the radicals, they put their country first and served on what was, by any fair estimate, a humanitarian mission to save the people of South Vietnam from the executions, reeducation camps, and oppression of Communism. In return, the radicals not only denounced them, but rewrote the history of their service and sacrifice. Veterans are, in fact, the most noble, selfless part of the sixties generation. And they deserve to be remembered that way.

Chapter Thirteen

☮

THE BIRTH OF THE *COUNTER* COUNTERCULTURE

A s we've seen, the 1960s was a conservative decade. It is undeniable, though, that statism—the idea that government knows best—was the dominant thinking in academia, in the Democratic Party, and even, despite the nomination of Barry Goldwater for president in 1964, in large swathes of the Republican Party.

What is less well known is how the 1960s saw the rise of a conservative counterculture that challenged statist ideas. Its roots can be traced far back, but for our purposes we can define this movement as beginning in 1944 with the publication of Friedrich Hayek's *The Road to Serfdom*.

Born and raised in Vienna, the economist and philosopher Friedrich von Hayek (1899–1992) was a former socialist whose thinking changed when he became a student of the free market economist Ludwig von Mises. Hayek was a faculty member at the London School of Economics when he wrote a long essay that would become a classic defense of the free market, *The Road to Serfdom*, which argued that central planning inevitably leads to tyranny.

A direct attack on Britain's Labour Party, the book quickly became a classic, establishing Hayek as a major conservative thinker. Although Hayek rejected the label of "conservative"—he thought of himself as a classical liberal—his book reaffirmed, as conservatism had long insisted, that economic and political freedom are indivisible.

Guess What?

❀ The most important intellectuals of the 1960s were on the political right

❀ Barry Goldwater's humiliating defeat paved the way for Ronald Reagan's victory in 1980

❀ Our politics today are the continuation of the ideological battles of the 1960s

☮ ☮ ☮ ☮ ☮ ☮ ☮ ☮ ☮ ☮ ☮ ☮ ☮ ☮

The Wisdom of Hayek

"We have progressively abandoned that freedom in economic affairs without which personal and political freedom has never existed in the past."

"Wherever the barriers to the free exercise of human ingenuity were removed, man became rapidly able to satisfy ever widening ranges of desire."

"Who can seriously doubt that the power which a millionaire, who may be my employer, has over me is very much less than that which the smallest bureaucrat possesses who wields the coercive power of the state and on whose discretion it depends how I am allowed to live and work?"

"Even the striving for equality by means of a directed economy can result only in an officially enforced inequality—an authoritarian determination of the status of each individual in the new hierarchical order."

—from *The Road to Serfdom*

Russell Kirk

Hayek's influence was felt even in a perhaps unlikely corner—that of a young American scholar who would become America's foremost traditionalist conservative, Russell Kirk (1918–94). Kirk's masterpiece, *The Conservative Mind*, published in 1953, is often credited with launching the postwar American conservative movement. Kirk upheld an Anglo-American conservatism that rested on a belief in a transcendent moral order, a respect for tradition, a defense of property rights, and a belief in dispersed power.

Kirk disdained leftist schemes to transform man and society. Such schemes, he argued, lead inevitably to tyranny. As Kirk elegantly put it,

"For the conservative, custom, convention, constitution, and prescription are the sources of a tolerable civil social order. Men not being angels, a terrestrial paradise cannot be contrived by metaphysical enthusiasts; yet an earthly hell can be arranged readily enough by ideologues of one stamp or another."[1]

Kirk's ideas went against the grain of the times. He rejected fashionable Marxist notions of a "classless society," and he denied that a better future could be built by "reason" and socialist planning. He also refuted the idea that religion was "the opiate of the masses." Instead, he staked out a lonely position in defense of social conservatism, whose essence he defined as "the preservation of the ancient moral traditions of humanity."[2] Kirk made the case that class divisions were a natural consequence of liberty and a guard against egalitarianism and uniformity; that experience was a better guide than ideology; and that the religion of the Bible was truer in its account of man and his nature than the utopian theories of leftist social engineers.

Milton Friedman

Another giant in the conservative movement was Milton Friedman (1912–60). Like Hayek (who would be his colleague at the University of Chicago), Friedman had started out on the Left, supporting the expansion of government during the New Deal.[3] Through empirical research, however, Friedman found that government intervention in the economy was often counterproductive, creating new problems even when it solved others. In opposition to John Maynard Keynes's support of interventionist policies and high spending to fight recessions, Friedman promulgated the philosophy of monetarism, which stressed the dangers of an excessive money supply. Based on his economic research, Friedman developed a long list of policy proposals that have become core conservative and libertarian positions, including low taxes, limited government regulation, school choice, and social security privatization.

Friedman's work was brought together in his landmark, 800-page study, *A Monetary History of the United States: 1867-1960*. Aside from academic works, he spread his ideas among a larger audience through radio and TV appearances, a regular *Newsweek* column, and by personally counseling leading politicians including Barry Goldwater, Richard Nixon, Ronald Reagan, and several advisors to British prime minister Margaret Thatcher.

Ayn Rand

Another key contributor to the emerging conservative philosophy was Ayn Rand (1905–82), a woman who, along with Hayek, was cited by Milton Friedman as a leading influence on his pro-market ideas.[4] Born in 1902 in St. Petersburg as Alisa Rosenbaum, Rand witnessed her father lose his chain of pharmacies after the Bolsheviks gained power in 1917. She fled to America in 1926 and worked for a time as a Hollywood script reader for the producer Cecil B. DeMille.

Are You Now or Have You Ever Been an Anti-Communist?

Rand wrote her first and what many consider her best novel, *We the Living*, in 1934, but she could not get it published until 1936 due to resistance from Communist sympathizers in the publishing industry. Like other anti-Communists in the 1930s, she found the Left had set up its own blacklist long before the McCarthy hearings.[5]

Moving to New York, Rand became a writer determined to warn America of the dangers of collectivism, which she had learned firsthand under the Bolsheviks. The seed of the idea behind the novel that would bring her worldwide fame, *The Fountainhead*, lay in a remark made to her by Marcella Bannert, an assistant producer in Hollywood. "Here's what I want out of life," Bannert said. "If nobody had an automobile, I would not want one. If automobiles exist and some people don't have them, I want an automobile. If some people have two automobiles, I want two automobiles."[6]

Rand's novel decried collectivism for inevitably destroying wealth and robbing people of their independent sense of will. *The Fountainhead* wove this theme into an over-the-top, sexually charged plot. The result was one of the most successful books ever published. By July 1945, it had sold 150,000 copies, and it would remain on the bestseller list for years.[7] Rand followed this up with another giant bestselling novel, *Atlas Shrugged*, which depicts a dystopian collectivist world in which the most talented and creative people have fled to a hold-out in South America. Taken together, Rand's works provided a powerful critique of the welfare state, holding out individualism as the core requisite of a productive, free society.

Objectivism in Two Sentences

"One cannot find a more eloquent symbol of man as a creator than a man who is a builder. His antithesis, the collectivists, are destroyers."

—**Ayn Rand** on the architect Howard Roark, the protagonist of *The Fountainhead* [8]

An atheist and supporter of legal abortion, Rand was not a conservative in many ways. Her graphic sexual writing was widely ridiculed, especially a sex scene in *The Fountainhead* between the hero and heroine that reads like a rape fantasy. She held grudges against conservatives who criticized her novels and even butted heads with other libertarians. Yet Rand's influence is undeniable, strengthening the libertarian streak in conservatism and communicating this message to a mass audience. She expounded her philosophy in TV appearances and in public speaking engagements, while her followers, calling themselves Objectivists, organized clubs to spread her ideas.

William F. Buckley Jr.

These various intellectual strands may have remained isolated outposts if not for one singular event: the founding of *National Review* in 1955 by William F. Buckley Jr. (1925–2008). Buckley ventured to create a magazine that would not simply critique liberalism (which held near monopoly status among intellectuals), but reject it outright in favor of a lively, intellectually rigorous conservatism. The magazine, he declared, "will forthrightly oppose the prevailing trend of public opinion; its purpose, indeed, is to change the nation's intellectual and political climate."[9]

Buckley's brainchild brought traditionalist, libertarian, and anti-Communist thinkers together, giving birth to a coherent intellectual tradition. Of course, there were tensions in the family; most notably, the magazine fiercely criticized Ayn Rand, beginning with a scathing 1957 review of *Atlas Shrugged* written by Whittaker Chambers, the Communist-turned-conservative who had famously—and correctly—identified high-ranking U.S. diplomatic official Alger Hiss as a Communist spy. Nevertheless, *National Review* became a bedrock institution of the conservative movement, attracting scores of writers who would provide the movement's intellectual and theoretical muscle over the ensuing decades. With his engaging personality, gentlemanly demeanor, and keen sense of humor, Buckley himself gave conservatism a new respectability through the auspices of *Firing Line*, a public affairs show he hosted for more than three decades beginning in 1966.

☮ ☮ ☮ ☮ ☮ ☮ ☮ ☮ ☮ ☮ ☮ ☮ ☮ ☮

A Conservative Manifesto

"Let's face it: Unlike Vienna, it seems altogether possible that did NATIONAL REVIEW not exist, no one would have invented it. The launching of a conservative weekly journal of opinion in a country widely assumed to be a bastion of conservatism at first glance looks like a work of supererogation, rather like publishing a royalist weekly within the walls of Buckingham Palace. It is not that, of course; if NATIONAL REVIEW is superfluous, it is so for very different reasons: It stands athwart history, yelling Stop, at a time when no one is inclined to do so, or to have much patience with those who so urge it."

—from the mission statement of *National Review*,

by **William F. Buckley Jr.**

Barry Goldwater lights the prairie fire

Thus, at the dawn of the 1960s, America remained an overwhelmingly conservative country culturally, yet it was just beginning to articulate a conservative philosophy in opposition to big government liberalism. As the intellectual argument developed, what was missing was a spark to transform the philosophy into a grassroots political movement. That spark was provided by Barry Goldwater (1909–98).

Born to a Jewish father and an Episcopalian mother, Goldwater had come from a wealthy family. When his father died, he dropped out of college to run the family's Phoenix department store. During World War II he served as a U.S. Army pilot and afterward served in the U.S. Air Force Reserve, reaching the rank of major general. An active Republican, Goldwater was elected in 1952 as a senator from Arizona, earning a reputation as a fiscal conservative, an anti-Communist, a crusader against corruption in organized labor, and a defender of states' rights and American sovereignty.

He defended these positions in the Senate at a time when the GOP was dominated by its liberal, northeastern wing. But after suffering a drubbing in the 1958 House and Senate elections, Republicans were ready for a new direction.[10]

Goldwater became a conservative icon with the publication of his manifesto, *The Conscience of a Conservative*, in April 1960. If one event marked the emergence of the modern popular conservative movement, this was it. Ghostwritten by *National Review* editor Brent Bozell, the book deftly weaved together the traditionalism of Kirk, the libertarianism of Freidman, and the anti-Communism of Hayek, and set forth a practical political philosophy that served as a blueprint for action.

The Conscience of a Conservative caught fire, quickly selling hundreds of thousands of copies and sparking a movement to draft Goldwater as the GOP's presidential nominee in 1960. That effort ended in disappointment with the nomination of Richard Nixon, though Goldwater electrified the Republican convention with a stirring call for conservatives to "get to work" and take back the party. Notably, the book was a sensation among college students, who started their own campaign to draft Goldwater as vice president. These students, many becoming politically active for the first time, created a conservative counterculture on America's college campuses through Young Americans for Freedom, founded in 1960.[11]

After Nixon lost the 1960 election to Kennedy, Republicans began looking ahead to the 1964 contest. As late as 1963 it was generally assumed that the GOP's next presidential nominee would be one of the party's many prominent liberals. The early favorite was New York governor Nelson Rockefeller, who enjoyed almost total support from the influential New York State Republican Party. In early 1963 even Goldwater believed Rockefeller would be the nominee, and he began contemplating Rockefeller's suggestion that he run as Rockefeller's vice president.

But Rockefeller's candidacy imploded in May when the governor revealed his intention to marry one of his office staffers, Margareta "Happy" Murphy, who was seventeen years younger than he and had just been divorced a month earlier.[12] The GOP's liberal establishment had three leading replacements: Pennsylvania governor William Scranton, Michigan governor George Romney, and for-mer Massachusetts senator Henry Cabot Lodge. Like John F. Kennedy, each had the patrician background that the media adored. But neither Scranton nor Romney nor Lodge could emerge as a clear front runner. That left Goldwater, whose supporters were enthusiasts and activists, with a clear path to the nomination.

A Book You're Not Supposed to Read

Upstream: The Ascendance of American Conservatism by Alfred S. Regnery (New York: Threshold Editions, 2008).

Goldwater became the Republican candidate for president and declared in his acceptance speech, "Extremism in the defense of liberty is no vice. And let me remind you also that moderation in the pursuit of justice is no virtue." Famous words that became a battle cry for his sup-porters, but were also turned against him by his opponents who tried to paint him as a bomb-happy extremist.

By any measure, Goldwater faced long odds in unseating President Lyndon Johnson, who still had the country's sympathy and support after the assassination of President Kennedy. On top of this, Johnson had an extremely valuable ally in the press corps, which was generally appalled by Goldwater's eagerness to upset the status quo. Of the many biased reports the press disseminated, the most damaging was a UPI story that ran during the primary reporting on remarks Goldwater had made on a TV show. Summarizing options the military had discussed for eradicat-ing the Ho Chi Minh trail, Goldwater had said, "There have been several suggestions made, I don't think we would use any of them. But defolia-tion of the forests by low-yield atomic weapons could well be done."[13] Clearly, the suggested use of atomic weapons came from the military, not Goldwater, who dismissed the idea even though he thought it technically feasible. But UPI reported Goldwater's comment as an explicit endorse-ment of a nuclear attack. Rockefeller seized on this to denounce Gold-water as a crazed warmonger, an image that the Johnson campaign later emphasized with the unquestioning connivance of the press.

This was ironic. Despite his strong anti-Communism, Goldwater was a critic of Johnson's military build-up in South Vietnam, insisting that America either act with full force against the Communist North Viet-namese or not get involved in the war at all. The press reacted by denouncing Goldwater as a warmonger, even as Johnson proceeded with

The Kind of Man He Was

"An ex-GI told me how he met [Barry Goldwater]. It was the week before Christmas during the Korean War, and he was at the Los Angeles airport try-ing to get a ride home to Arizona for Christmas, and he said that there were a lot of servicemen there and no seats available on the planes. Then a voice came over the loudspeaker and said, 'Any men in uniform wanting a ride to Arizona, go to runway such-and-such,' and they went down there, and there was this fellow named Barry Goldwater sitting in his plane. Every day in the weeks before Christmas, all day long, he would load up the plane, fly to Ari-zona, fly them to their homes, then fly back over to get another load."

—**Ronald Reagan**, on Barry Goldwater[17]

his gradual, but eventually massive, escalation of America's military commitment in Southeast Asia.[14]

The UPI story was one of many fraudulent press attacks on Goldwater. Two of the worst abuses were perpetrated by CBS News. In one, interviewer Eric Sevareid conducted a two-hour interview in which Goldwater repeatedly expressed his contempt for the far-right John Birch Society. The broadcast, however, included just one sentence of his remarks, in which Goldwater noted that the Birchers' activities were not unconstitutional.[15] In another story, later repeated by the *New York Times*, CBS's Daniel Schorr made the preposterous assertion that Goldwater was planning to lecture Neo-Nazi groups and to visit Hitler's summer home on an upcoming trip to West Germany.[16]

The media's demonization of Goldwater was effective; the impression spread that he was dangerous, even mentally unstable, and liable to trigger a nuclear war. The Johnson campaign exploited these fears, most notoriously with its "Daisy" commercial. The ad showed a little girl counting to ten as she plucked petals from a daisy, which was interrupted by a technician's voice counting down to zero, followed by a fiery atomic bomb blast. It ended with President Johnson's voice admonishing, "These are the stakes: to make a world in which all of God's children can live, or to go into the dark. We must either love each other, or we must die." Such raw emotionalism and fear-mongering, without even the pretense of a rational argument, was part and parcel of the Johnson campaign.

In the end, Goldwater could not overcome the coldly calculated assaults of the Johnson camp and the press. He also suffered from liberal Republicans' resentment at the conservatives' ascendency, which was most starkly expressed in a letter to Goldwater from Scranton's aides denouncing the senator's "absurd and dangerous positions" and calling his convention delegates a "flock of chickens whose necks will be wrung at will."[18] Goldwater went on to lose the election in an historic landslide, winning just six states.

Out of the ashes

The liberal media, unsurprisingly, was overjoyed at Goldwater's defeat. According to the *New York Times*, "Barry Goldwater not only lost the presidential election...but the conservative cause as well."[19] While this may have been liberal conventional wisdom back then, it would become clear in time that the death of conservatism was greatly exaggerated.

For the moment, however, conservatives were in for a rough ride. Over the next four years, the Johnson administration presided over a massive expansion of the welfare state. Conservatives got little relief with the 1968 election of Richard Nixon. In fact, Nixon took Johnson's tax-and-spend, big government liberalism, and added his own compassionate conservative agenda to it. Under Nixon, Aid to Families with Dependent Children, food stamps, and the alphabet soup list of other federal welfare programs all continued to expand rapidly, with many growing even faster than they had under Johnson.[20]

The excessive spending was not confined to welfare. For political reasons, Nixon supported expanded agriculture payments to wheat farmers, bigger price supports to dairy farmers, and other government interventions against market forces. As a result of his profligate spending, by fiscal 1971, the federal deficit had risen to $23.2 billion,[21] and Nixon went on to average more than $18 billion per year in deficits over the course of his presidency.[22] In his most dramatic act of contempt for free enterprise, between 1971 and 1973 Nixon imposed wage and price controls in a failed attempt to reduce inflation.

Nixon's presidency ended the 1960s on a disappointing note for conservatives. And there was not much reason for optimism throughout the following decade, as big government continued to grow under presidents Nixon and Gerald Ford, and America become mired in economic stagnation (or "stagflation") and foreign policy retreat under President Jimmy Carter.

But in 1980, the seeds that Goldwater had planted two decades before suddenly bloomed with the election of Ronald Reagan. Reagan first came to political prominence in 1964 with his rousing "Time for Choosing" speech in support of Goldwater's candidacy. The victory of his 1980 campaign, in which he emphasized the conservative trinity of small government, anti-Communism, and traditional moral values, was the culmination of years of work beginning with the grassroots movement that formed around Goldwater in 1960 and 1964. With Reagan's election, the modern conservative movement had produced its first president.

Reagan's election took many by surprise, but really it was the vindication of the real counterculture of the 1960s—the counterculture that was actually constructive rather than destructive, that actually represented America as it really was and really wanted to be—the conservatism of the crew cuts who opposed the long hairs, of those who answered their nation's call rather than those who dodged it, of those who thought there was more to life than sex, drugs, and rock 'n' roll—namely, personal responsibility, fidelity, and family.

The battle between this divided generation goes on; in fact, it is the dividing line of American politics today. Our future depends on which side comes out on top.

ACKNOWLEDGMENTS

I suppose it's good to keep one's acknowledgments under one page. So let me merely list first a few people I know personally and then a few people I don't.

I'm most grateful to my editor, Jack Langer. Jack appears to work harder than James Brown and, to the best of my knowledge, without the aid of drugs. He did an amazing job of cutting a much longer manuscript down to an appropriate size, while never being anything but positive and upbeat. Few know how brilliant he is. More ought to.

An ingenious friend who was active in the sixties Left but smart enough to leave it, Jonathan Rubinstein, inspired my interest in the period. I thank him.

I'm also appreciative of the friendship I've had and comments I've received from a number of smart people while writing the book: Paul C. Craig, Rick Brookhiser, Deroy Murdock, Jonathan Funke, John Zmirak, Fred Campano, and Russ and Chris Jenkins.

I'm ever more grateful to have the family I do: my brother Daniel, sister Sarah, my mother Susan Fox, stepfather H. Jonathan Fox, and late and much missed stepmother Diane Alington.

In addition, I'm appreciative of quite a few authors whose books greatly influenced this one. Foremost among these folks is Charles Murray, author of *Losing Ground*, a book that is absolutely worth reading for anyone who hasn't yet read it. I also found the works of Thomas Sowell, Mark Moyar, and Gerard J. DeGroot particularly helpful. Thanks to them.

Finally, my thanks to all the other terrific people at Regnery, especially Harry Crocker and Elizabeth Kantor.

NOTES

Introduction

1. Alex Ross, *The Rest is Noise: Listening To The Twentieth Century* (New York: Farrar Straus and Giroux, 2007), 382.

2. Joseph Murrells, *Million Selling Records: From the 1900s to the 1980s, An Illustrated History* (New York: Arco Publishing, 1985), 94–185. The figures for *My Fair Lady* combine those for the more famous 1956 stage soundtrack with the film soundtrack. Both went platinum.

Chapter One

1. Bettina Aptheker, *Intimate Politics: How I Grew Up Red, Fought for Free Speech, and Became a Feminist Rebel* (California: Seal Press, 2006), 55.

2. Mario Savio, "Mario Savio Graduation Speech, Sidwell Friends School, June 10, 1988"; available online at: http://www.writing.upenn.edu/~afilreis/50s/savio-speech.html.

3. Ibid.

4. California Legislature, "Thirteenth Report of the Senate Fact-Finding Subcommittee on Un-American Activities—California"; available online at: http://content.cdlib.org/xtf/view?docId=kt4w1003q8&brand=calisphere&doc.view=entire_text.

5. Dotson Rader, *Blood Dues* (New York: Alfred A. Knopf, 1973), 13.

6. G. Louis Heath, ed. *Vandals in the Bomb Factory* (New Jersey: Scarecrow Press, 1976), 97 and 174–75.

7. Malcolm X and Alex Haley, *The Autobiography of Malcolm X* (New York: Random House, 1973), 324.

8. James T. Paterson, *Great Expectations: The United States, 1945-1974* (New York: Oxford University Press, 1996), 645.

9. "Who We Are," Students for a Democratic Society, http://students-forademocraticsociety.org/node/6?q=node/4.

10. Caitlan Millat and Corky Siemaszko, "'Revolution' at New York University ends with cafeteria liberated, arrests of students," *New York Daily News*, February 20, 2009; available online at:
http://www.nydailynews.com/news/ny_crime/2009/02/20/2009-02-20_revolution_at_new_york_university_ends_w.html; and "Protesting NYU Students Offered Lighter Punishment," NY1.com, February 27, 2009; available online at: http://www.ny1.com/content/top_stories/94667/protesting-nyu-students-offered-lighter-punishment/Default.aspx.

11. "Comedy Gold: The End of the NYU Occupation," *Hot Air*, February 23, 2009; available online at: http://hotair.com/archives/2009/02/23/comedy-gold-the-end-of-the-nyu-occupation/.

12. Dotson Rader, *Blood Dues*, 4.

13. Peter Collier and David Horowitz, *Destructive Generation: Second Thoughts About the 60s* (USA: Encounter Books, 1989), 101.

14. David Horowitz, *The Professors: The 101 Most Dangerous Academics In America* (Washington, D.C.: Regnery, 2006), 125.

15. Cathy Wilkerson, "Fugitive Days," book review, *Zmag* magazine, December 1, 2001.

16. Dinitia Smith, "No Regrets for a Love of Explosives; In a Memoir of Sorts, a War Protester Talks of Life With the Weathermen," *New York Times*, September 11, 2001; available online at:
http://www.nytimes.com/2001/09/11/books/no-regrets-for-love-explosives-memoir-sorts-war-protester-talks-life-with.html.

17. Tony Blankley, *American Grit* (Washington, D.C.: Regnery, 2009), 167.

18. James A. Michener, *Kent State: What Happened and Why* (Random House, New York, 1971), 99–105.

19. Ibid., 16.

20. Ibid., 26–27.

21. Ibid., 204–7.

22. Ibid., 56–61, 407.

23. Joseph Kelner, *The Kent State Coverup* (New York: Harper & Row, 1980), 66.

24. James A. Michener, *Kent State*, 387.

25. "Spy Fired Shot that Changed West Germany," *New York Times*, May 26, 2009.

26. William A. Gordon, *The Fourth of May: Killings and Coverups at Kent State* (Buffalo, New York: Prometheus Books, 1990), 104.

27. I. F. Stone, *The Killings at Kent State: How Murder Went Unpunished* (New York: A New York Review Book, 1971), 26.

28. Philip Caputo, *13 Seconds: A Look Back at the Kent State Shootings* (New York: Penguin Group, 2005), 164–67.

29. David Horowitz, *The Professors*, 13.

30. Ibid., 183–85.

31. Ibid., 202–05.

32. Ibid., 212–14.

33. http://www.gradeinflation.com/.

34. Angela Davis, UC Santa Cruz faculty webpage, http://histcon.ucsc.edu/faculty/davis.html.

35. David Horowitz, *The Professors*, 241–44.

36. Ibid., 315–18; for more information on Orville Schell, see http://orvilleschell.com/biography.htm.

37. Young America's Foundation, "Top Ten Bizarre and Most Politically Correct College Courses," *Human Events*; available online at: http://www.humanevents.com/article.php?id=18926.

38. Everett Carll Ladd Jr. and Seymour Martin Lipset, *The Divided Academy: Professors and Politics* (New York: McGraw-Hill, 1975), 57.

39. David Lehman, "Paul de Man: The Plot Thickens," *New York Times*, May 24, 1992; available online at: http://www.nytimes.com/1992/05/24/books/paul-de-man-the-plot-thickens.html.

Chapter Two

1. Hofferth, Kahn, and Baldwin, National Opinion Research Center, University of Chicago.

2. Helen Gurley Brown, *Sex and the Single Girl* (New York: Bernard Geis Associates, 1962), 1–4.

3. Ibid.

4. Daniel Horowitz, *Betty Friedan and the Making of the Feminine Mystique: The American Left, the Cold War, and Modern Feminism* (Amherst, MA: University of Massachusetts Press, 1998), 230.

5. Judith Hennessee, *Betty Friedan: Her Life* (New York: Random House, 1999), 81–82.

6. Betty Friedan, *The Feminine Mystique* (New York: W. W. Norton & Company, 1997), 382–99.

7. Daniel Horowitz, *Betty Friedan and the Making of the Feminine Mystique*, 181–82.

8. Judith Hennessee, *Betty Friedan*, 190; and Betty Friedan, *Life So Far: A Memoir* (New York: Simon & Schuster, 2000), 88.

9. Daniel Horowitz, *Betty Friedan and the Making of the Feminine Mystique*, 230.

10. As quoted in Judith Hennessee, *Betty Friedan*, 240.

11. Carolyn G. Heilbrun, *The Education of a Woman – The Life of Gloria Steinem* (New York: Ballantine Books, 1995), 12–25.

12. Judith Hennessee, *Betty Friedan,* 153.

13. Ibid., 156–57.

14. Carolyn G. Heilbrun, *The Education of a Woman*, 267.

15. Susan Oliver, *Betty Friedan: The Personal Is Political* (New York: Library of American Biography, Pearson, Longman, 2008), 125.

16. Judith Hennessee, *Betty Friedan*, 177.

17. "Men and their Discontents," Salon.com; http://208.17.81.135/col/pagl/1997/10/14frames.html.

18. Alice Echols, *Shaky Ground: The Sixties and Its Aftershocks* (New York: Columbia University Press, 2002), 99.

19. Chris Kraus and Sylvère Lotringer, eds. *Hatred of Capitalism: A Semiotext(e) Reader* (New York: Semiotext(e) 2001), 335.

20. Tammy Bruce, *The New American Revolution* (New York: William Morrow, 2005), 100–1.

21. John R. Lott Jr., *Freedomnomics: Why the Free Market Works and Other Half-Baked Theories Don't* (Washington, D.C.: Regnery, 2007), 121–22.

22. Sharon Jayson, "Divorce declining, but so is marriage," *USA Today*; available online at: http://www.usatoday.com/news/nation/2005-07-18-cohabit-divorce_x.htm.

23. Flora Davis, *Moving The Mountain: The Women's Movement in America Since 1960*, (Urbana, IL: University of Illinois Press, 1997), 160-61.

24. Mary Turner, *The Women's Century: A Celebration of Changing Roles* (Ann Arbor, MI: National Archives, 2006), 118.

25. James Q. Wilson, *The Marriage Problem: How Our Culture Has Weakened Families* (New York: Harper Collins, 2002), 175–76

26. Flora Davis, *Moving the Mountain*, 289 and 350–51.

Chapter Three

1. Raymond Arsenault, *Freedom Riders: 1961 and the Struggle for Racial Justice* (New York: Oxford University Press, 2006), 27.

2. Ibid., 47.

3. Ibid., 143–49.

4. Thomas Sowell, *Affirmative Action Around The World: An Empirical Study* (CT: Yale University Press, 2004), 119.

5. Thomas Sowell, *Civil Rights: Rhetoric or Reality?* (New York: William Morrow & Company, 1984), 65.

6. Thomas Sowell, *Affirmative Action Around The World*, 118.

7. Thomas Sowell, *Civil Rights*, 49.

8. Ibid.

9. Philip F. Rubio, *A History of Affirmative Action: 1619-2000* (Jackson, MS: University of Mississippi Press, 2001), 119.

10. Thomas Sowell, "'Affirmative Action' Reconsidered," in Barry R. Gross, ed. *Reverse Discrimination* (Buffalo, New York: Prometheus Books, 1977), 120–23.

11. As quoted in Philip F. Rubio, *A History of Affirmative Action*, 140–41.

12. As quoted in John David Skrentny, *The Ironies of Affirmative Action: Politics, Culture, and Justice in America* (Chicago: The University of Chicago Press, 1996), 70.

13. Nicolaus Mills, "Affirmative Action on The Ropes," *Dissent*, reprinted in Robert Emmet Long, ed. *Affirmative Action* (New York: The H. W. Wilson Company, 1996), 46.

14. Nathan Glazer, *Affirmative Discrimination: Ethnic Inequality and Public Policy* (Cambridge: Harvard University Press, 1987), 44–45.

15. Terry Eastland, *Ending Affirmative Action: The Case For Colorblind Justice* (New York: Basic Books), 119–20.

16. Ibid., 60–61.

17. Thomas Sowell, *Affirmative Action Around The World*, 149.

18. Charles Murray, "Affirmative Racism" in Nicolaus Mills, ed. *Debating Affirmative Action: Race, Gender, Ethnicity, and The Politics of Inclusion* (New York: Delta Trade Paperbacks, 1994), 198.

19. Officially sanctioned racial discrimination in the guise of "affirmative action" had advanced so far by the 1980s that the University of Texas eventually was admitting black students with combined SATs of 900 (on a 400–1600 scale) and rejecting Asians with scores as high as the 1500s. Blacks at Berkeley in 1988 entered with an SAT average of 952 as against a white average of 1232 and an Asian average of 1254. Not surprisingly, 70 percent of all black admittees never graduated. At Georgetown Law School the average black Law School Admission Test Score came to be below that of any white admittee. See Thomas Sowell, *Affirmative Action Around The World*, 131–32 and 146–47.

20. Taylor Branch, *Pillar of Fire: America in the King Years, 1963-1965* (New York: Simon & Schuster, 1968), 334–36.

21. John Fabanjong, *Understanding the Backlash Against Affirmative Action* (Huntington, New York: Nova Science Publishing, 2001), 17.

22. John David Skrentny, *The Ironies of Affirmative Action*, 75.

23. Kenneth R. Timmerman, *Shakedown: Exposing the Real Jesse Jackson* (Washington, D.C.: Regnery, 2002), 7.

24. Ibid.

25. Louis De Caro Jr., *On The Side of My People: A Religious Life of Malcolm X* (New York: New York University Press, 1996), 47.

26. Ibid., 59–60, 65.

27. Malcolm X with Alex Haley, *The Autobiography of Malcolm X* (New York: Random House, 1973), 339–53.

28. Ibid., 324.

29. David Hilliard, with Keith and Kent Zimmerman, *Huey: Spirit of the Panther* (New York: Thunder's Mouth Press, 2006), 12.

30. Peter Collier and David Horowitz, *Destructive Generation: Second Thoughts About the Sixties* (New York: Encounter Books, 1989), 158.

31. David Hilliard, *Huey*, 13–14.

32. Ibid., 28.

33. Ibid., 31–34.

34. Ibid., 156, quoting Huey Newton, *Hidden Traitor*.

35. Jewel was reiterating a statement previously made by Stokely Carmichael. See Rebecca Klatch, *A Generation Divided: The New Left, the New Right, and the 1960s* (CA: University of California Press, 1999), 208.

36. Peter Collier and David Horowitz, *Destructive Generation*, 161.

37. Ibid., 162–64.

38. Peter Collier and David Horowitz, *Destructive Generation*, 162.

39. Ibid., 38–66.

40. Hugh Pearson, *The Shadow of the Panther: Huey Newton and the Price of Black Power In America* (Cambridge, MA: Da Capo Press, 1995), 311–15.

41. John Kifner, "Eldridge Cleaver, Black Panther Who Became G.O.P. Conservative, Is Dead at 62," *New York Times*, May 2, 1998; available online at: http://www.nytimes.com/1998/05/02/us/eldridge-cleaver-black-panther-who-became-gop-conservative-is-dead-at-62.html.

42. Peter Collier and David Horowitz, *Destructive Generation*, 162.

43. John Fabanjong, *Understanding the Backlash Against Affirmative Action*, 72.

44. Gerald Horne, *Fire This Time: The Watts Uprising and the 1960s* (Charlottesville, VA: University Press of Virginia, 1995), 58–60.

45. Ibid., 66.

46. John Fabanjong, *Understanding the Backlash Against Affirmative Action*, 72.

47. Ibid.

48. Edward C. Banfield, *The Unheavenly City Revisited* (Boston, MA: Little Brown and Company, 1974), 211.

49. Mark Hamilton Lytle, *America's Uncivil Wars: The Sixties Era from Elvis to the Fall of Richard Nixon* (New York: Oxford University Press, 2006), 251.

50. David A. Sears and John B. McConahay, *The Politics of Violence: The New Urban Blacks and the Watts Riots* (Boston, MA: Houghton Mifflin Company, 1973), 84.

51. Ibid., 98.

52. Dan La Botz, *Cesar Chavez and la Causa* (New York: Pearson Longman, 2006), 82.

53. Ibid., 91.

54. Ibid., 49.

Chapter Four

1. Rachel Carson, *Silent Spring* (Boston, MA: Houghton Mifflin, 1962), 266–75.The author is quoting the head of the Dutch Plant Protection Service.

2. Ronald Bailey, "Silent Spring at Forty," *Reason*, June 12, 2002.

3. Justin Martin, *Nader: Crusader, Spoiler, Icon* (New York: Basic Books, 2003), 148–49.

4. "Ralph Nader Asks if Barack Obama Will Be an Uncle Tom," http://www.youtube.com/watch?v=ibsP6XN2dIo.

5. Thomas Sowell, "Ralph Nader's Glittering Record," *Capitalism* Magazine, March 3, 2004; available online at: http://www.capmag.com/article.asp?ID=3547.

6. David Sanford, *Me & Ralph: Is Nader Unsafe For America?* (Washington: A New Republic Book, 1976), 18.

7. "Ralph Nader Enters Presidential Race," CNN.com; available online at: http://www.cnn.com/2008/POLITICS/02/24/nader.politics/index.html.

Chapter Five

1. Dave McAleer, *The All Music Book of Hit Singles* (San Francisco, CA: Miller-Freeman, 1994), 59–137.

2. As quoted in Frederic Dannen, *Hit Men: Power Brokers and Fast Money Inside the Music Business* (New York: Vintage Books, 1991), 73.

3. Joseph Murrells, *Million Selling Records: From the 1900s to the 1980s, An Illsutrated History* (New York: Arco Publishing, 1985), 94–185. The fig-

ures for *My Fair Lady* combine those for the more famous 1956 stage soundtrack with the film soundtrack. Both went platinum.

4. Sean Egan, ed. *100 Albums That Changed Music – and 500 Songs You Need To Hear* (London: Constable & Robinson, 2006).

5. Nathan Rabin, "The A.V. Club Interviews Gene Simmons," The A.V. Club, March 20, 2002; available online at: http://www.avclub.com/articles/gene-simmons,13759/.

6. As quoted in Nadya Zimmerman, *Counterculture Kaleidescope: Musical and Cultural Perspectives on Late Sixties San Francisco* (Ann Arbor, MI: University of Michigan Press, 2008), 136.

7. Ibid.

8. Laura Mansnerus, "Timothy Leary, Pied Piper of Psychedelic 60's, Dies at 75," June 1, 1996, *The New York Times,* A1; avaialble online at: http://www.nytimes.com/1996/06/01/us/timothy-leary-pied-piper-of-psychedelic-60-s-dies-at-75.html.

9. Douglas Martin, "Sandy Lehmann-Haupt, 59, One of Ken Kesey's Busmates," obituary, *New York Times*, November 3, 2001; available online at http://www.nytimes.com/2001/11/03/arts/sandy-lehmann-haupt-59-one-of-ken-kesey-s-busmates.html.

10. http://www.cdc.gov/ncipc/factsheets/poisoning.htm.

11. Clinton Heylin, *Bob Dylan: Behind the Shades—A Biography* (New York: Summit Books, 1991), 26.

12. Ibid., 39.

13. Ibid., 30.

14. Frederic Dannen, *Hit Men: Power Brokers and Fast Money Inside the Music Business*, 67.

15. Clinton Heylin, *Bob Dylan*, 153–54.

16. Ibid., 47 and 295.

17. John Blaney, *Beatles for Sale: How Everything They Touched Turned to Gold* (UK: Outlook Press, 2008), 43–44.

18. Joe Steussy, *Rock and Roll: Its History and Stylistic Development* (New Jersey: Prentice-Hall, 1990), 125–32.

19. David Wild, "They Can't Take That Away From Me: Frank Sinatra and His Curious But Close Relationship with The Rock'n'Roll Generation,"

in Jeanne Fuchs and Ruth Prigozy, eds. *Frank Sinatra: The Man, The Music, The Legend* (Rochester, New York: University of Rochester Press, 2007), 37.

20. Susannah Cahalan, "Give Beast A Chance: 'Imagine' Lennon As Cruel Misogynist," *The New York Post*, October 12, 2008; available online at: http://www.nypost.com/seven/10122008/news/nationalnews/give_beast_a_chance_133215.htm. The article's source is Philip Norman's 2008 biography *John Lennon: A Life*, and is quoting an account by Yoko Ono that was given by her to the biographer.

21. Joe Steussy, *Rock and Roll*, 116.

22. As quoted in Christopher Andersen, *Jagger Unauthorized* (New York: Delacorte Press, 1993), 106.

23. Ibid., 108–23.

24. Dora Loewenstein and Philip Dodd, eds. *According to the Rolling Stones* (San Francisco, CA: Chronicle Books, 2003), 88–90.

25. Christopher Andersen, *Jagger Unauthorized*, 249.

26. Ibid., 271.

27. http://ralphellison.net/more.html

28. Christopher Andersen, *Jagger Unauthorized,* 8.

29. Ibid., 7.

30. Ibid., 3–13.

Chapter Six

1. Irving Settel, *A Pictorial History of Television* (New York: Frederick Ungar Publishing Co., 1983), 160–61, 195.

2. "Entertainment Scene Presents: 20 Most Popular TV Shows Each Year in the 1960s," http://www.entertainmentscene.com/top_tv_shows_60s.html.

3. Janet Maslin, "Film View; The Sad Tale of a Hustler is Reissued," *New York Times*, February 20, 1994; available online at: http://www.nytimes.com/1994/02/20/movies/film-view-the-sad-tale-of-a-hustler-is-reissued.html.

4. Aldo Tassone, *Antonioni* (Paris: Flammarion Press, 2007), 13.

Chapter Seven

1. "Zodiac Movie Review,"
http://barinya.com/australia/zodiac_review.htm.

2. Penelope Byrde, *A Visual History of Costume: The Twentieth Century* (New York: Drama Book Publishers, 1992), 113.

3. Marian Fowler, *The Way She Looks Tonight* (New York: St. Martin's Press, 1996), 288–94.

4. Ibid., 305.

5. Nadya Zimmerman, *Counterculture Kaleidoscope*, 60.

6. Ibid., 100–1.

Chapter Eight

1. Hugh Sidey, "Why We Went to the Moon," *Time* Magazine, July 25, 1994; available online at:
http://www.time.com/time/magazine/article/0,9171,981167,00.html.

2. Ronald Bailey, "Mars: the Red-Tape Planet," *Reason Online*, January 14, 2004; available online at:
http://www.reason.com/news/show/34746.html.

3. Gerard J. DeGroot, *Dark Side of the Moon: The Magnificent Madness of the American Lunar Quest* (New York: New York University Press, 2006), 90–91, 123.

4. Ibid., 72–98.

5. "Sputnik and the Crisis That Followed," U.S. Centennial Flight Commission; available online at:
http://www.centennialofflight.gov/essay/SPACEFLIGHT/Sputnik/SP16.htm.

6. Gerard J. DeGroot, *Dark Side of the Moon*, 124 and 87–88.

7. Ibid., 119–20.

8. Ibid., 123.

9. Ibid.

10. Ibid.

11. Ibid., 126.

12. Based on personal interview with an Ivy League Astrophysics Professor who wishes to remain anonymous.

13. Tom Wolfe, *The Right Stuff* (New York: Farrar, Straus & Giroux, 1979), 78 and 180–81.

14. Ibid., 127–28.

15. Ibid., 419–21.

16. Gerard J. DeGroot, *Dark Side of the Moon*, 15.

17. Michael J. Neufeld, *Von Braun: Dreamer of Space, Engineer of War* (New York: Alfred A. Knopf, 2007), 175–80.

18. Cadbury, 337.

19. Ibid., 335.

20. Gerard J. DeGroot, *Dark Side of the Moon*, 24–26.

21. Cadbury, 317–38.

22. David West Reynolds, *Apollo: The Epic Journey to the Moon* (New York: Harcourt, 2002), 85.

23. Ibid., 92.

Chapter Nine

1. Jim Newton, *Justice For All: Earl Warren And The Nation He Made* (New York: Riverhead Books, 2006), 93.

2. Ibid., 123.

3. Ibid., 131; and Bill Hosokawa, *Nisei: The Quiet Americans* (CO: University Press of Colorado, 2002), 287.

4. Bill Hosokawa, *Nisei*, 287–88.

5. Ibid., 287.

6. Ibid., 288.

7. Ibid., 373.

8. Jim Newton, *Justice for All*, 186.

9. Kevin Gutzman, *The Politically Incorrect Guide to the Constitution* (Washington, D.C.: Regnery, 2007), 195.

10. John Fund, "Miers Remorse: Conservatives are right to be skeptical," October 10, 2005; available online at:
http://www.opinionjournal.com/diary/?id=110007384.

11. Paul Finkelman and Melvin I. Urofsky, *Landmark Cases of the United States Supreme Court* (Washington, D.C.: CQ Press, 2003), 281.

12. Robert H. Bork, *Coercing Virtue: The Worldwide Rule of Judges* (Washington, D.C.: AEI press, 2005), 69.

13. Paul Finkelman and Melvin I. Urofsky, *Landmark Cases of the United States Supreme Court*, 302.

14. Bernard Schwartz and Stephan Lesher, *Inside the Warren Court, 1953–69* (New York: Doubleday, 1983), 219.

15. National Center for Policy Analysis, "Handcuffing the Cops: Miranda's Harmful Effects on Law Enforcement," Study #218, August 1998.

16. Bernard Schwartz, *A History of the Supreme Court* (New York: Oxford University Press, 1993), 274.

17. Schwartz with Lesher, 139.

18. Jim Newton, *Justice for All*, 494–95, 502.

19. Bruce Allen Murphy, *Wild Bill: The Legend and Life of William O. Douglas, America's Most Controversial Supreme Court Justice* (New York: Random House, 2003), 432.

20. Ibid., 376.

21. Paul Finkelman and Melvin I. Urofsky, *Landmark Cases of the United States Supreme Court*, 405.

Chapter Ten

1. Peter Carlson, "Another Race To the Finish," *The Washington Post*, November 17, 2000, p. A1; available online at: http://www.washingtonpost.com/ac2/wp-dyn/A36425-2000Nov16?language=printer.

2. Earl Mazo and Stephen Hess, *Richard Nixon: A Political and Personal Portrait* (New York: Harper & Brothers, 1968).

3. Peter Carlson, "Another Race To the Finish," p. A1.

4. From "US Presidents and Election Fraud," http://rangevoting.org/PresFraud.html.

5. Ibid.

6. Robert D. Novak, *The Prince of Darkness: 50 Years Reporting in Washington* (New York: Crown Forum, 2007), 178; and "US Presidents and Election Fraud," http://rangevoting.org/PresFraud.html.

7. Robert A. Caro, *The Years of Lyndon Johnson: The Means of Ascent* (New York: Vintage Books, 1991), 307.

8. Ibid., 265.

9. Ibid., 314.

10. Ibid., 341.

11. Ibid., 391–94.

12. Ibid., 312–13.

13. Ibid., 321.

14. Peter Carlson, "Another Race To the Finish," A1.

15. Patricia Sullivan, Obituaries: "Earl Mazo, 87; Richard Nixon Biographer," *The Washington Post*, February 17, 2007, p. C7; available online at: http://www.washingtonpost.com/wp-dyn/content/article/2007/02/17/AR2007021701356.html.

16. Anthony DePalma, *The Man Who Invented Fidel: Castro, Cuba and Herbert L. Matthews of The New York Times* (PA: Perseus Books, 2006), 161.

17. Volker Skierka, *Fidel Castro: A Biography* (Cambridge: Polity Press, 2004), 50.

18. Robert E. Quirk, *Fidel Castro* (New York: W.W. Norton & Company, 1993), 132.

19. Ibid., 132.

20. Robert E. Quirk, *Fidel Castro*, 15-16.

21. Humberto E. Fontova, *Fidel: Hollywood's Favorite Tyrant* (Washington, D.C.: Regnery, 2005), 117.

22. Robert E. Quirk, *Fidel Castro,* 248.

23. Humberto E. Fontova, *Fidel*, 118-19.

24. Robert E. Quirk, *Fidel Castro*, 349.

25. Ibid., 350.

26. Ibid., 351.

27. Humberto E. Fontova, *Fidel*, 39.

28. Robert E. Quirk, *Fidel Castro,* 348.

29. Ibid., 428.

30. Ibid.

31. Philip Nugus, "Weapons Races: Nuclear Bomb," Television documentary for the Military Channel & Nugus/Martin Productions, LTD.

32. "The Week," *National Review*, December 26, 2008, p. 12.

33. Humberto E. Fontova, *Fidel*, 24.

34. Robert E. Quirk, *Fidel Castro*, 438–43.

35. Ibid., 441.

36. As quoted in Robert D. Novak, *The Prince of Darkness*, 368.

37. Martin F. J. Prachowny, *The Kennedy-Johnson Tax Cut: A Revisionist History* (Ontario: Edward Elgar, 2000), 194.

38. Robert Sobel, *The Last Bull Market: Wall Street in the 1960s* (New York: Norton, 1980), 175.

39. Robert Sobel, *The Big Board: A History of the New York Stock Exchange* (Frederick, MD: Beard Books, 2000), 340, 359–67; John Brooks, *The Go-Go Years – The Drama and Crashing Finale of Wall Street's Bullish 60s* (New York: Allworth Press, 1998), 113; and Robert Sobel, *The Last Bull Market*, 72.

40. Robert Sobel, *The Last Bull Market*, 172.

41. Martin F. J. Prachowny, *The Kennedy-Johnson Tax Cut*, 198.

42. Robert Sobel, *The Last Bull Market*, 196.

43. This is when adjusted for inflation. John Dennis Brown, *101 Years on Wall Street: An Investor's Almanac*, 88.

44. John Dennis Brown, *101 Years on Wall Street: An Investor's Almanac* (Englewood Cliffs, NJ: Prentice Hall, 1991), 90.

45. Obituary "John N. Mitchell Dies at 75: Major Figure in Watergate," *New York Times*, November 10, 1988, p. A1; available online at: http://www.nytimes.com/1988/11/10/obituaries/john-n-mitchell-dies-at-75-major-figure-in-watergate.html.

46. John Brooks, *The Go-Go Years*, 136.

47. Charles R. Geisst, *Wall Street: A History* (New York: Oxford University Press, 1997), 287.

48. Ibid., 293.

49. Richard Reeves, *President Kennedy: Profile of Power* (New York: Touchstone Books, 1994), 24.

50. Ibid., 242–43.

51. "The health and Medical History of President John Kennedy," http://www.doctorzebra.com/prez/g35.htm.

52. Richard Reeves, *President Kennedy*, 24.

53. Arthur Schlesinger Jr., *A Thousand Days: John F. Kennedy in the White House* (New York: Houghton Mifflin Co, 1965), 1–936.

54. Richard Reeves, *President Kennedy*, 147.

55. "The McNeil-Lehrer News Hour," November 18, 2002.

56. Seymour Hersh, *The Dark Side of Camelot* (Boston: Little Brown and Company, 1997), 240–43.

57. Ibid., 100–6.

58. Dave Reitzes, "The JFK 100: One Hundred Errors of Fact and Judgment in Oliver Stone's JFK," http://www.jfk-online.com/jfk100menu.html.

59. Vincent Bugliosi, *Reclaiming History: The Assassination of John F. Kennedy* (New York: W. W. Norton & Company, 2007), 1371–75.

60. Ibid., 1370–71.

61. Richard Reeves, *President Kennedy*, 41.

62. Ibid., 295.

Chapter Eleven

1. Charles Murray, *Losing Ground: American Social Policy, 1950-1980* (New York: Basic Books, 1981), 65.

2. Ibid., 48.

3. Ibid., 47.

4. Ibid., 14.

5. Ibid., 73–76.

6. Ibid., 38.

7. Frances Fox Piven and Richard A. Cloward, *Regulating The Poor: The Functions of Public Welfare* (New York: Vintage Books, 1993), 186.

8. Fred Siegel, *The Future Once Happened Here: New York, D.C., L.A. and the Fate of America's Big Cities* (New York: The Free Press, 1997), 49.

9. Charles Murray, *Losing Ground*, 157–66.

10. Andrew Bernstein, "The Welfare State Versus Values and the Mind," http://www.andrewbernstein.net/articles/7_welfarestate.htm.

11. Charles Murray, *Losing Ground*, 115.

12. Ibid., 120.

13. Ibid., 112–19.

14. Ibid., 169.

15. Ibid., 150–52.

16. Elliott Currie, *Reckoning: Drugs, The Cities and the American Future* (New York: Hill and Wang, 1993), 20.

17. Erica Goode, "For Users Of Heroin, Decades Of Despair," *The New York Times,* May 22, 2001; also at *Science Times*, p.1.

18. Joseph A. Califano Jr., *High Society: How Substance Abuse Ravages America and What to Do about It* (New York: Perseus Books, 2007), 112–13.

19. John R. Lott Jr. and Sonya D. Jones, "Abortion Rate Among Black Women Far Exceeds Other Groups," FoxNews.com, April 9, 2008, and http://www.abort73.com/?/print/22/.

20. "Quotes about Inflation," http://www.gaia.com/quotes/topics/inflation.

21. Eric F. Goldman, *The Tragedy of Lyndon Johnson* (New York: Alfred A. Knopf, 1969), 165.

Chapter Twelve

1. Ho Chi Minh, *The Prison Diary of Ho Chi Minh*, trans. Aileen Palmer with an Introduction by Harrison Salisbury (New York: Bantam Books, 1971), ix–xvi.

2. Noam Chomsky and Edward S. Herman, *After The Cataclysm: Postwar Indochina and The Reconstruction of Imperial Ideology* (Boston, MA: South End Press, 1979), 28.

3. David Halberstam, *The Best and The Brightest* (New York: Ballantine Books, 1992), 105.

4. Anthony James Joes, *The War for South Vietnam, 1954–1975* (Greenwich, CT: Praeger Publishers, 2001), 11.

5. Jean Lacouture, *Ho Chi Minh: A Political Biography*, trans. Peter Wiles (New York: Random House, 1968), 31, quoting Ho Chi Minh, "The Path Which Led Me To Leninism" from the July 1960 issue of *L'echo du Vietnam*.

6. As quoted in Mark Moyar, *Triumph Forsaken: The Vietnam War, 1954–1965* (New York: Cambridge University Press, 2006), 8.

7. Pierre Brocheux, *Ho Chi Minh: A Biography*, trans. Claire Duiker (New York: Cambridge University Press, 2007), 17, 20, 33.

8. Jean Lacouture, *Ho Chi Minh*, 44.

9. Pierre Brocheaux, *Ho Chi Minh*, 24.

10. Ibid., 28–29.

11. Sophie Quinn-Judge, *Ho Chi Minh: The Missing Years: 1919–1941* (Berkeley, CA: University of California Press, 2002), 155; and Mark Moyar, *Triumph Forsaken*, 10.

12. Mark Moyar, *Triumph Forsaken*, 11.

13. Anthony James Joes, *The War for South Vietnam, 1954–1975*, 36. Communist sources, however, suggest that the death toll was "only" around 32,000, albeit with tens of thousands more beaten and sent to concentration camps. See Mark Moyar, *Triumph Forsaken*, 62.

14. Ibid., 10.

15. Ibid., 11.

16. Anthony James Joes, *The War For South Vietnam, 1954-1975*, 12–13.

17. Stanley Karnow, *Vietnam: A History* (NewYork: Penguin, 1997), 233.

18. Mark Moyar, *Triumph Forsaken*, 17–18.

19. Ibid., 19.

20. Pierre Brocheaux, *Ho Chi Minh*, 75.

21. Mark Moyar, *Triumph Forsaken*, 21.

22. Anthony James Joes, *The War for South Vietnam, 1954–1975*, 19.

23. Mark Moyar, *Triumph Forsaken*, 17–18.

24. Pierre Brocheaux, *Ho Chi Minh*, 103–4.

25. Mark Moyar, *Triumph Forsaken*, 18.

26. Jean Lacouture, *Ho Chi Minh*, 107.

27. Mark Moyar, *Triumph Forsaken*, 79.

28. Michael Lee Lanning and Dan Cragg, *Inside the VCA and the NVA: The Real Story of North Vietnam's Armed Forces* (New York: Fawcett Columbine, 1992), 203.

29. Ibid.

30. Ibid.

31. Anthony James Joes, *The War for South Vietnam, 1954–1975*, 146.

32. Michael Lee Lanning and Dan Cragg, *Inside the VCA and the NVA*, 46.

33. Ibid., 238.

34. Ibid., 68.

35. Anthony James Joes, *The War for South Vietnam, 1954–1975*, 55.

36. Ibid., 99.

37. Ibid., 55.

38. Michael Lee Lanning and Dan Cragg, *Inside the VCA and the NVA*, 69.

39. See Daryl C. Smith, "U.S. Navy Seabees: We Build, We Fight," *All Hands* Magazine, January 2008; and Marc Leepson, "The Heart and Mind of USAID's Vietnam Mission," American Foreign Service Association, Wash-

ington, D.C., 2000. See also Rufus Phillips, *Why Vietnam Matters* (Annapolis, MD: Naval Institute Press, 2008).

40. "Nguyen Ngoc Loan, 67, Dies; Executed Viet Cong Prisoner," *New York Times*, July 16, 1998.

41. Eddie Adams, "Eulogy," *Time*, July 27, 1998.

42. Stanley Karnow, *Vietnam*, 480.

43. Mark W. Woodruff, *Unheralded Victory: The Defeat of the Viet Cong and the North Vietnamese Army, 1961-1973* (New York: Presidio Press, 2005), as cited in Harry Crocker, *Don't Tread on Me*, 427–28, N. 11.

44. Stanley Karnow, *Vietnam*, 480.

45. Anthony James Joes, *The War for South Vietnam, 1954–1975*, 99.

46. Ibid.

47. Ibid.

48. Ibid., 100, quoting Samuel Popkin, "The Village War" in *Vietnam as History*, ed. Peter Braestrup (Washington, D.C.: University Press of America, 1984).

49. Anthony James Joes, *The War for South Vietnam, 1954–1975*, 92.

50. Ibid., 100.

51. Dominic Sandbrook, *Eugene McCarthy: The Rise and Fall of Post-War American Liberalism* (New York: Alfred A. Knopf, 2004), 184.

52. Ibid., 132.

53. Ibid.

54. Michael Lee Lanning and Dan Cragg, *Inside the VCA and the NVA*, 119; and Anthony James Joes, *The War for South Vietnam, 1954–1975*, 136.

55. Michael Lee Lanning and Dan Cragg, *Inside the VCA and the NVA*, 238.

56. Ibid., 121.

57. Harry Crocker, *Don't Tread on Me* (New York: Crown Forum, 2006), 377.

58. Stanley Karnow, *Vietnam*, 672, quoting the memoirs of General Tran Van Tra.

59. Harry Crocker, *Don't Tread on Me*, 377.

60. Anthony James Joes, *The War for South Vietnam, 1954–1975*, 135.

61. Ibid.

62. "Ron Dellums," http://www.absoluteastronomy.com/topics/Ron_Dellums.

63. David Horowitz, "Horowitz's Notepad: An Enemy Within," September 19, 2001, FrontPageMagazine.com, http://frontpagemagazine.com/readArticle.aspx?ARTID=21218.

64. Jimmy Breslin, "Is Washington Ready For Bella Abzug? Is Anybody?" *New York Magazine*, October 5, 1970, available at: http://nymag.com/news/politics/48260/; and "Spartacus Educational," http://www.spartacus.schoolnet.co.uk/USAabzug.htm.

65. John Gizzi, "Em-Bella-shing Her Past," *Human Events*, May 1, 1998; available at: http://findarticles.com/p/articles/mi_qa3827/is_199805/ai_n8788538/.

66. Keith Windschuttle, "The Hypocrisy of Noam Chomsky," *The New Criterion*, May 2003; available at: http://www.newcriterion.com/articles.cfm/chomsky-windschuttle-1733.

67. Michael Lee Lenning and Dan Cragg, *Inside the VCA and the NVA*, 120–21.

68. John Prados, *The Blood Road: The Ho Chi Minh Trail and The Vietnam War* (New York: John Wiley & Sons Inc., 1999), 299.

69. Philip Short, *Pol Pot: The History of A Nightmare* (London: John Murray, 2004), 85.

70. Ibid., 99, 101.

71. Ibid., 96.

72. Ibid.

73. Ibid., 104.

74. Ibid., 146.

75. Ibid.

76. Ibid., 221. See also David P. Chandler, *Brother Number One: A Political Biography of Pol Pot* (Boulder, CO: Westview Press, 1992), 95.

77. Susan Stern, *With the Weatherman: The Personal Journal of a Revolutionary Woman* (New Jersey: Rutgers University Press, 1975), 31.

78. Ibid.

79. Susan Stern, *With the Weatherman*, 32–33.

80. Ibid., 32–33.

81. "Abbie Hoffman Biography," http://www.focusdep.com/biographies/Abbie/Hoffman.

82. Don Feder, "The American Taliban's Plea For Mercy," FrontPage Magazine.com, October 4, 2004; available at: http://www.frontpagemag.com/readArticle.aspx?ARTID=11142.

83. Rennie Davis, introduction to Charles Cameron, ed. *Who is Guru Maharaj Ji?* (New York: Bantam Books, 1973).

Chapter Thirteen

1. Russell Kirk, *The Conservative Mind: From Burke to Eliot* (Washington, D.C.: Regnery, 2001), xv–xvi.

2. Ibid., v.

3. Lanny Ebenstein, *Milton Friedman: A Biography* (New York: Palgrave MacMillan, 1977), 43.

4. Ibid., 151.

5. Jeff Britting, *Ayn Rand* (New York: Overlook Duckworth, 2004), 41.

6. Ibid., 50.

7. Ibid., 71.

8. Ibid., 51.

9. Alfred S. Regnery, *Upstream: The Ascendance of American Conservatism* (New York and London: Threshold Editions, 2008), 63.

10. Lee Edwards, *Goldwater: The Man Who Made a Revolution* (Washington, D.C.: Regnery, 1995), 105–13.

11. Alfred S. Regnery, *Upstream*, 86–88, 91–92.

12. Robert D. Novak, *The Prince of Darkness*, 105.

13. Lee Edwards, *Goldwater*, 168.

14. Ibid., 363–66.

15. Ibid., 176.

16. Ibid., 177.

17. Excerpt from Ronald Reagan, "A Time For Choosing," see: http://www.reagan.utexas.edu/archives/reference/timechoosing.html.

18. Edwards, *Goldwater*, 258–59.

19. Ibid., xiii.

20. Stephen E. Ambrose, *Nixon: The Triumph of A Politician* (New York: Simon and Schuster, 1989), 327.

21. Ibid., 432.

22. "U.S. Federal Deficits and Presidents," http://home.adelphi.edu/sbloch/deficits.html.

INDEX